I DO

A GRACE-FILLED GUIDE TO NEW COVENANT MARRIAGE

JEANNINE DE SWARDT

This book is a mentoring tool designed to help couples build their marriage on the Finished Work of Jesus Christ and the grace of the New Covenant. It is not intended as professional counseling.

This book will be most beneficial when done with a mentor couple using the Mentor's Guide. Couples are encouraged to seek Godly pastoral counsel when needed.

ISBN: 978-1-972677-02-5

First Edition: 2026

Publisher: Adventure Press

To every young couple who desires a marriage that reflects the love of Christ for His bride — may you discover the deep joy of resting in what Jesus has already finished on the cross.

I also want to lovingly acknowledge my husband. Thank you for walking with me every day in this beautiful adventure called marriage. Your constant love, support, and dedication mean more to me than words can say. Thank you for your wise guidance and faithful help in bringing this guide to life. I could not have done it without you.

Dear precious Couple,

Congratulations! You are stepping into one of the most beautiful and significant seasons of your life. As you prepare for marriage, my heart's desire is that you would experience the joy and freedom of a truly grace-filled New Covenant marriage — a marriage built not on performance or striving, but on the Finished Work of Jesus Christ and the Father's unconditional love.

This book, *I Do – A Grace-Filled Guide to New Covenant Marriage*, is designed as a practical mentorship guide to walk you through nine meaningful sessions. Each session combines biblical truth, real-life stories, discussion questions, and simple exercises that will help you build a strong foundation together.

While you can certainly go through this material on your own as a couple, I believe you will receive the greatest benefit when you use it in conjunction with a mature mentor couple and the Mentor Guide. Having an older, wiser couple walk alongside you, listening, sharing their own stories, and gently guiding the conversations, adds depth, accountability, and encouragement that is hard to find any other way.

A Note About This Course

Every marriage is unique because every person is uniquely created by God. In this book you will find some general differences between how men and women often communicate and relate. These are helpful patterns, but they are not rules. Sometimes the roles may be reversed in your relationship — and that is perfectly okay!

This course is not about fitting into boxes. It is about growing in love and understanding through the Finished Work of Jesus. Answer the exercises honestly, listen to each other with grace, and let the Holy Spirit show you how to love one another in your own special marriage. There is no condemnation here—only freedom to grow closer.

Welcome to the journey. I'm cheering for you.

With love and expectation,

Jeannine de Swardt

TABLE OF CONTENTS

The Heart of Marriage

For this cause shall a man leave his father and mother, and shall be joined unto his wife, and they two shall be one flesh.

This is a great mystery: ... (Eph 5:31,32a)

What Is Marriage

Marriage is a God-ordained union in which two individuals become one flesh in Christ: "For this reason a man shall leave his father and mother and be joined to his wife, and the two shall become one flesh. This is a great mystery, but I speak concerning Christ and the church" (Ephesians 5:31-32, NKJV).

Under the New Covenant, this oneness is a living reflection of Christ's finished work on the cross. In Him we are already complete and fully accepted (Colossians 2:10). Growth and fruitfulness in marriage flow not from striving, but from abiding together in Christ (John 15:4-5), allowing His grace to produce unity even as we celebrate our individuality.

1. SPIRITUAL UNION

Before God and through God a spiritual oneness is formed. God instituted marriage to help us overcome egocentricity and to mirror His commitment to His children.

In the eyes of the law, marriage is often viewed as a contract—performance-oriented, built on the equation 1 + 1 = 2. Each person gives 50 percent, keeps 50 percent, and includes conditional clauses and escape routes. In the eyes of God, however, marriage is not a contract but a covenant. A covenant is an eternal promise, sealed with vows, the exchange of tokens, and sometimes blood. It speaks of total commitment: two individuals becoming one new unit—one flesh.

Biblical tokens of covenant illustrate this beautifully: exchanging robes (giving reputation and life), exchanging belts (covering each other's weaknesses and fighting each other's battles), and the sacrifice (sealed in blood). In marriage this total union is sealed through sexual consummation, symbolizing the complete giving of self. It is total giving and receiving—no part withheld. Therefore, it can only be monogamous.

It is important that you receive your mate as God's provision for you. In Genesis 2:18 the Lord God said, "It is not good that man should be alone; I will make a helper comparable to him." Adam's response was immediate: "This is now bone of my bones and flesh of my flesh; she shall be called Woman, for she was taken out of Man" (Genesis 2:23).

This acceptance flows from the finished work of the cross: we are fully loved and accepted by God (Ephesians 1:6), so we can receive our spouse without performance demands. We love because He first loved us (1 John 4:19). It is not about earning love but resting in Christ's perfect love for us.

Why does God take marriage so seriously? Because marriage mirrors the unbreakable New Covenant love of Christ for His church, sealed by His blood, not our performance (Ephesians 5:31-32). The world should look at Christian marriages and marvel, "So that's how much Jesus loves the church!"

A grace-filled marriage doesn't happen through human effort alone. It flows as we rest in Christ's finished work and allow the Holy Spirit to produce His fruit—love, commitment, and unity—in us (Galatians 5:22). Total commitment becomes our joyful response to His unchanging covenant love, not a heavy burden we carry in our own strength.

Marital union is intimate—so intimate that the Bible describes it as two becoming one flesh (Genesis 2:24). A healthy marriage combines closeness with separateness. Don't give up your uniqueness and individuality; that is often what first attracted your partner.

2. **COGNITIVE UNION** (Meeting of the minds)

Cognitive unity includes the following:

2.1 Views On The World, Life And Humanity

View of God: Most marital partners share a fundamental opinion about faith in God and the sovereignty of Jesus Christ. Denominational differences, theological differences, even though you may be in the same church, and differing values and norms can threaten marital union. It is best not to marry a non-Christian, the bible warns against being unequally yoked.

Life View: This can differ substantially due to dissimilar backgrounds and personalities, for example: optimistic / pessimistic; trusting / distrusting; frugal / spendthrift, etc. Should these differences be mishandled, marital union can be threatened.

Views on Humanity: Substantial differences with regard to attitude and behavior toward others can also threaten marital union.

Please note: It is often wrongly assumed that marital unity demands and all-inclusive, cognitive unity. This is a myth, an unrealizable dream. One does not have to agree or feel the same about everything. Thought patterns should overlap but must never be all-inclusive. The marital partner's own identity, thought framework and individuality must be acknowledged and respected. Christian partners should at least agree to leave room for each other's uniqueness (also regarding thinking patterns) without continual attempts to change each other's point of view. Agree to disagree. (NOT *Tolerate* to disagree.) Don't try and clone yourself!

2.2 Unrealistic And / Or Wrong Expectations

Many partners have unrealistic expectations of marriage arising either from their cultural or their personal background. It is very important that you discuss your expectations of marriage with your partner and ensure that you have the same picture in your minds. We are not the same, we do not think alike!

Partners need to face the myths of marriage with honesty. For too long marriage has been saddled with unrealistic expectations and misguided assumptions.

The golden rule is: **NEVER ASSUME ...... EXPLORE!**

We are going to discuss five of the most common and most harmful misconceptions about marriage, i.e.

Myth 1: We expect exactly the same things from Marriage

What we anticipate seldom occurs, what we least expect generally happens – especially in marriage. Saying "I do" brings with it a host of conscious and unconscious expectations that aren't always fulfilled.

Most misguided expectations fall into two major categories: unspoken rules and unconscious rules. Bringing both of them out into the open can save years of wear and tear on a young marriage.

Unspoken Rules

You are invited to lunch at your in-law's house on a sweltering August day. Everybody had been playing in the pool, and when lunch is announced you dish up your food and wait for grace to be said. All the other men have put their shirts on and the family exchange meaningful glances of which you are totally unaware. On the way home your wife bursts out: "How could you be so rude to my family?" You are flabbergasted not having a clue what she is talking about. The wife interprets your behavior (eating without a shirt) as downright rude and disrespectful to her and her family. You, on the other hand don't understand her intensity. In your parents' house it was never an issue unless were sitting at a table to eat.

Everyone lives by a set of rules that is rarely spoken but always known. Needless to say, unspoken rules become more vocal when our spouse "breaks" them. Let us illustrate this with the following example:

In this incident the husband had broken a rule that he didn't know existed, and the wife most probably discovered a rule that she hadn't put into words. Both had their own ideas about what was acceptable and it never occurred to either that their expectations could be so different. Each one became irritated by the other's unspoken expectations and frustrated that the other did not live by the same rules.

Avoid an unnecessary blow-up by learning to discuss your secret expectations and making your silent rules known.

Unconscious Roles

The second source of mismatched expectations involves the unconscious roles that you and your partner fall into, almost involuntarily. Without realizing it, a bride and groom are drawn into acting out roles that they adopt from a blend of their personalities, family backgrounds and marital expectations. Let us illustrate by the following example:

Husband and wife return from honeymoon and begin to set up house, arranging furniture, hanging paintings and curtains. He: "Where do you want this table?" She: "I don't know; where do you think it should go?" After this scenario has been repeated 3 times, he says exasperated: "Just tell me where to put it!" Before they know it, they are having their first fight.

Unconsciously they are acting out roles they had observed in their families of origin. The wife's father, a handyman with a decorator's eye, would re-arrange the furniture every now and then. Her mom simply assisted him when he asked for help, not really interested in interior decorating. The husband's dad, on the other hand, is a busy executive with no interest in decorating the house. His mom is the one who organized the home.

In these illustrations both husband and wife took on their "assigned" roles as husband and wife, displaying acquired behavior from childhood, each wondering why the other wasn't pulling his or her own weight. Marriage combines two very different behavioral and role expectations. Once you are aware of the roles you tend to take in a script that was written by the role models you grew up with, you can write your own script for your marriage. Failure to do so can threaten your marital union.

The expectations you bring to your partnership can make or break your marriage. Don't believe the myth that you and your partner automatically come with the same expectations for marriage. Evaluate your expectations in the light of the following different kinds of marriages:

- The Traditional Marriage

In this model there is a clear division of roles. The husband is primarily the provider and financial center of the home, while the wife focuses on the care of the household and children. She is often seen as the emotional heart of the family.

This can be a stable and satisfying marriage when both partners genuinely desire these roles. However, it can also create challenges: the husband may tie his identity too tightly to his work and unintentionally neglect emotional connection, while the wife may feel unfulfilled or suppressed if she has gifts and dreams beyond the home. A subtle power imbalance can develop if roles become rigid rather than flexible expressions of love. Under grace, couples can enjoy the strengths of this model without being trapped by its limitations, remembering that their deepest identity and security come from Christ, not from how well they perform traditional roles (Colossians 2:10).

- The Companionate Marriage

Here both husband and wife have careers or significant responsibilities outside the home, and they share child-rearing and household tasks more equally. It is often described as a "horizontal" or partnership model.

This can be a busy but deeply satisfying marriage when both partners value teamwork and mutual contribution. The potential pitfall is that life becomes so full of responsibilities that romance and couple-time slowly disappear. The marriage can begin to feel more like a well-run business partnership than a passionate covenant. Under grace, couples in this model are reminded to protect intentional time together, not out of duty, but because they are already secure in Christ's love. They can rest in the truth that their worth is not earned by how efficiently they divide chores or careers, but by who they already are in Him (Ephesians 1:6). Making couple-time becomes a joyful overflow rather than another item on the to-do list.

- The Romantic Marriage

This is the "just the two of us" marriage. The couple is deeply in love, highly affectionate, and often so focused on each other that they have little room for others, including, at times, their own children.

The beautiful side is that children growing up in this home often feel secure seeing their parents visibly in love. The danger is that the couple can become so wrapped up in one another that children feel like intruders or outsiders. Under grace, this marriage can flourish when the couple remembers that their deepest love and completion come from Christ, not from each other. They are free to enjoy their romance without making it an idol, and they can open their hearts to others (including children) because they are already filled by His unchanging love. Passion and exclusivity become gifts to steward, not the entire foundation of their identity.

- The Rescue Marriage

In this model, one or both partners enter the relationship hoping the other will rescue them from loneliness, past pain, an unhappy home, or personal brokenness. It often feels intense and "meant to be" at first.

This is one of the most dangerous foundations for marriage because it places an impossible burden on a spouse to be savior and healer — a role that belongs only to Jesus. Under grace, couples are invited to examine their motives honestly. The good news is that true healing and wholeness are already provided in Christ's finished work (Isaiah 53:5; Colossians 2:10). No spouse can fix what only Jesus can heal. When both partners rest in the truth that they are already complete in Him, they can enter marriage from fullness rather than lack. The relationship then becomes a place where two healed (or healing) people walk together, pointing each other back to the real Rescuer instead of trying to rescue each other.

- The New Covenant Marriage (Grace-Centered Marriage)

This is the kind of marriage God designed under the New Covenant—a living picture of Christ's unbreakable love for His church.

In a New Covenant marriage, both husband and wife know they are already fully loved, accepted, complete, and righteous in Christ (Colossians 2:10; Ephesians 1:6; 2 Corinthians 5:21). They do not look to each other to complete them—Jesus has already done that perfectly through His finished work.

They enter marriage from fullness, not lack. Secure in Christ's love, they are free to love without demands, scorekeeping, or fear of rejection. Their marriage becomes a covenant of grace, not a contract of rules. "I will never leave you nor forsake you" (Hebrews 13:5) echoes in their commitment to each other, just as Christ never leaves His bride.

They are heirs together of the grace of life (1 Peter 3:7), growing side by side as the Holy Spirit produces love, joy, peace, and patience from within. Roles are shared with grace and flexibility. Differences become opportunities for grace to shine. Forgiveness flows freely because they remember how much they have been forgiven (Ephesians 4:32).

This is the marriage God invites every couple into—one that flourishes not because we try harder, but because it rests on what Christ has already done.

Myth 2: Everything good in our relationship will automatically get better.

The truth is that many things do improve in relationships, but some things get more difficult. Every successful marriage requires facing necessary losses and adjustments. In choosing to marry, you give up certain freedoms and idealized images, entering a mourning process for what was (single life, childhood roles, the 'perfect' version of your partner you first saw).

The good news under the New Covenant is this: the fading of initial romance doesn't mean the end of love—it opens the door to deeper, grace-based intimacy. Christ's finished work assures us we are already fully loved and accepted (Ephesians 1:6), so we can move from idealizing our spouse to receiving them as they are, just as Christ receives us. Disenchantment becomes an opportunity for the Holy Spirit to produce real, enduring love (Galatians 5:22–23) rather than performance-based romance. Facing reality in grace allows marriage to reflect Christ's unchanging covenant love, not fleeting feelings.

Myth 3: Marriage will heal my brokenness and make me happy.

Many people marry hoping to escape loneliness, pain, or past hurts (the "rescue" dynamic). But marriage is not a substitute for the deep inner healing that only comes through Christ's finished work on the cross. Jesus is our Healer (Isaiah 53:5), and true wholeness is found in Him alone (Colossians 2:10).

Your broken areas: self-doubt, unworthiness, past wounds, remain after the wedding because marriage doesn't produce character transformation; the Holy Spirit does, as you rest in grace (2 Corinthians 3:18). If you are an unhappy single person, you will carry that into marriage, unless you allow Christ's grace to heal you first.

Marriage can reflect Christ's healing: as you receive unconditional love from Him, you become equipped to love your spouse freely, and mutual grace-filled acceptance can create a safe space where the Spirit works. But never look to your spouse to be your healer or life preserver, that role belongs to Jesus.

To prepare: Be honest about your brokenness. Have you sought Christ's healing through His Word, prayer, and perhaps godly counsel?

Observe your potential mate: Are they resting in Christ's wholeness, or seeking you to fix them? Under grace, marriage becomes a partnership of two complete-in-Christ individuals growing together, not two halves becoming one through effort."

Myth 4: "My spouse will make me whole".

The old saying "opposites attract" often stems from people being drawn to those who seem to "complete" them. But Proverbs 27:17 ("iron sharpens iron") points to growth through relationship, not completion.

Under the New Covenant, you are already complete in Christ (Colossians 2:10). Marriage does not make you whole; it reveals and reflects the wholeness you already have in Him.

The opposite, rugged independence, also misses grace, as it denies the beauty of mutual support in Christ.

True interdependence flows from individual security in Christ's finished work: high self-esteem rooted in being loved and accepted by God (not performance), choosing to stand together as "heirs together of the grace of life" (1 Peter 3:7). Each partner has wholeness in Christ, yet chooses to grow, support, and sharpen the other by grace. This creates a strong couple identity without losing individuality—exactly as God designed in the mystery of one flesh (Eph. 5:31–32).

Myth 5: "I will change him/her after we are married"

This is the biggest lie that the devil can dish up! If there is anything in your partner's personality or if he/she has habits that you find offensive and difficult to live with: if they are **<u>not</u>** willing or able to change these before the marriage, they will **<u>not</u>** change them after you are married. In fact, they will most probably become worse as he/she will not have to put their best foot forward to impress you anymore!

Change in character and habits comes not by human effort or nagging, but by the transforming power of the Holy Spirit as we behold Christ (2 Corinthians 3:18). Under grace, we love and accept our spouse as they are in Christ, trusting God to work in them, just as He works in us. Trying to "fix" your partner before or after marriage undermines grace and breeds resentment.

Beware of these myths. They are poison to any marriage.

2.3 Shared Norms And Values

We need to be patient in deciding who to marry and really look at whether they would be the best spiritual partner for us as well as life partner – because when we marry God intends for us to be joined with them spiritually for the rest of our lives. And if they don't live out that which God values as being important, that could forever greatly affect our lives (and our future children and so many others) in very negative ways.

It is imperative that husband and wife are both born again. In **2 Corinthians 6:14** we read: **"Do not be yoked together with unbelievers. For what do righteousness and wickedness have in common? Or what fellowship can light have with darkness?"** This scripture is very clear and to disregard it is courting disaster. God clearly expects a believer to marry a believer.

Not only is it important that your partner is a believer, but it is also important that they are more or less on the same spiritual level as you are and equally passionate about serving God and living life to the glory of God.

For Christian marriages Biblical norms and values are **non-negotiable**. This often causes the Christian marriage to stand in conflict with many norms upheld by society. Make sure your values correspond and plan how you are going to handle compromising situations.

Under the New Covenant, we pursue biblical values not to earn God's favor (already ours in Christ), but because His grace transforms us to live them out (Titus 2:11-12).

2.4 The Quest For Meaning

God created man intending him to find meaning in his Creator, therefore man in essence always searches for meaning and will never find true peace of mind without God. This quest can threaten marital happiness. Man is questioning by nature and wants to know why things happen to him, why his partner is behaving in a certain way. Subconsciously he tries to find a cause, to give reason to, to find a scapegoat. Behavior is blamed on something or someone else (usually the partner).

"I love you because you..." is less of a problem than "I drink because you ..." but may communicate conditional love and acceptance.

The naming and blaming game threaten marital union. It causes false feelings of guilt, disregards own feelings of guilt and could eventually result in separation, if not dealt with.

3. SHARED ENVIRONMENTAL FACTORS

3.1 Living Space

The most universal stress factor in marriages is differences over household issues. Physical space may easily become a battleground of control, power and authority

Once again, established patterns of behavior, learned from the family of origin are involved here, for instance, general roles around the house, financial management, and the biggie – the way in which special days such as birthdays, anniversaries and Christmas are to be celebrated. These issues need to be discussed **before** marriage as it can threaten marital unity.

3.2 Making Early Adjustments

As we submit to God and each other in our marriages, we are being conformed to Christ's image (Romans 8:29). We adjust not in our strength, but by relying on His grace (2 Corinthians 12:9). Humility flows from seeing ourselves as God sees us and agreeing with His assessment (Philippians 2:3).

The solution to handling issues of adjustment lies in regarding your relationship as more important than your individual values and desires. If you hold on tightly to what you want, you'll never get to the point where you understand that the wellbeing of the overall relationship is what ultimately matters.

Here are some points to remember as you make adjustments in your relationship:

- **Recognize that adjustments are inevitable. Every married couple has to deal with the grains of sand in their shoes.** It's one hundred percent normal. If you realize up front that you'll have to make changes in your behavior and learn to tolerate frustrating traits in your spouse, your attitude will be more in line with what James wrote: **"Consider it all joy, my brethren, when you encounter various trials" (James 1:2).** He said to consider it all joy when you encounter trials, not if you encounter them.

- Understand that adjustments are a normal, everyday part of marriage. They are not a burden or a competition. We don't keep score with thoughts like, "I did it last time, so now it's your turn." Instead, we willingly adjust and grow because we love our spouse and value our oneness. When we are stretched, we grow—and that growth happens naturally as we rest in Christ's love and allow the Holy Spirit to produce His fruit in us.
- Ask God for wisdom on how to live with this person who's different from you. Instead of trying to change your spouse and correct all of the bad habits, how can you accept the situation or adjust yourself? Marriage may be an institution, but it isn't a reformatory.
- Be more concerned about your own rough spots than those of your spouse. Jesus said we should take the log out of our own eye before trying to take the speck out of someone else's eye. That's truly advice made in heaven for marriage. If I'm not willing to make changes, how can I expect my partner to change.
- Make a commitment to work through the inevitable adjustments. The apostle Paul provided guidelines for handling adjustment problems when they come your way: "Do nothing from selfishness or empty conceit, but with humility of mind let each of you regard one another as more important than himself" (Philippians 2:3). That's a description of a grace-based marriage, giving your partner room to be different.

FOOD FOR THOUGHT

"We love because he first loved us." 1 John 4:19

Because Christ has already loved you perfectly and completely through the cross, you are free to love your future spouse from fullness, not from lack. Rest in His finished work and watch His love flow through you into your marriage.

EXERCISE ONE

YOUR PERSONAL TEN COMMANDMENTS

This exercise is designed to help you uncover some of your unspoken rules. Try to articulate some of the unspoken rules you grew up with. Take your time to think it over. These unspoken rules are generally so ingrained that we are rarely aware of them. Once both of you have articulated your "personal ten commandments", share them with each other. Are there rules you would like to change? Take a moment to discuss how unspoken rules might affect your marriage.

Anytime you have a fight or disagreement, ask yourself: "Is this fight a result of one of us breaking an unspoken rule?" If so, add that rule to your list and discuss with your partner how you will handle that situation in the future.

1. ______________________________

2. ______________________________

3. ______________________________

4. ______________________________

5. ______________________________

6. ______________________________

7. ______________________________

8. ______________________________

9. ______________________________

10. ______________________________

EXERCISE TWO

MAKING YOUR ROLES CONSCIOUS

Listed below are a number of chores or life tasks that will need to be handled by you or your partner. To make your unconscious understanding of roles conscious, first indicate how your parents handled these tasks. Then indicated how you would like to divide up the tasks, according to your understanding of your own and your partner's interest, time and abilities. After discussing with your partner, put your final decision of who will do what in the last column, and be prepared to renegotiate when your circumstances change.

	Your Mother	Your Father	Both Parents	You	Your Partner	Both of you	Final Decision
Providing income	o	o	o	o	o	o	________
Staying home with children	o	o	o	o	o	o	________
Handling finances	o	o	o	o	o	o	________
Garden work	o	o	o	o	o	o	________
Car Maintenance	o	o	o	o	o	o	________
Laundry	o	o	o	o	o	o	________
Cleaning	o	o	o	o	o	o	________
Food preparation	o	o	o	o	o	o	________
Grocery shopping	o	o	o	o	o	o	________
Caring for pet	o	o	o	o	o	o	________
Scheduling social events	o	o	o	o	o	o	________
Maintaining ties with friends or relatives	o	o	o	o	o	o	________
Planning vacations	o	o	o	o	o	o	________
Initiating sex	o	o	o	o	o	o	________
Decorating the house	o	o	o	o	o	o	________
Initiating discussions about the relationship	o	o	o	o	o	o	________
Keeping the house neat and orderly	o	o	o	o	o	o	________
Disciplining the children	o	o	o	o	o	o	________
Shopping for other needs	o	o	o	o	o	o	________

Note: We believe that some of these tasks (such as disciplining children or initiating sex) must be shared in order for the couple to have a strong relationship, but in reality, many of these tasks may fall disproportionately to the husband or the wife because of unspoken assumptions or circumstances. Use this list periodically to discuss how you are doing and readjust your roles or assignments if you need to.

1. When you are sick, how much sympathy will you require? How would you expect your spouse to take care of you?

____

____

____

2. How much time do you expect to spend with your friends after you are married?

____

____

____

____

3. How will you relate to opposite sex friends once you are married? Will it be acceptable to phone, text or meet alone? What about social media?

____

____

____

____

4. How often would you like to eat out?

____

____

____

____

____

5. How important are family mealtimes to you? Do you want to sit at the table of in front of the Television? What about electronics (phones, tablets, etc.) at the dinner table?

6. How do you feel about screen time when you are spending quality time together?

7. Where do you want to live? (City/suburb/countryside)? Do you want to live in an apartment or house?

8. What is your understanding of "cleaning the house"?

9. Do you want children? If so, how many?

10. What would you do if you cannot conceive children on your own?

____

11. How involved should a father be in the upbringing of his children? Be specific about your expectations, for e.g. he should bathe the children every night, etc.

12. How will you discipline your children? Do you envision sharing the responsibility?

13. How often do you want to invite people to your home? Would you expect to be consulted beforehand?

14. What role will television play in your lives and what guidelines will you have?

15. What hobbies or recreational pursuits will you pursue individually?

Together:

How often:

16. What about a girls/guys night out?

17. Who will take spiritual leadership in the home and what do you think this means?

18. When and how often will you pray and study the Bible together?

19. Where will you attend church and what will your involvement be?

20. Where will you go and what will you do during holidays? How will you decide?

EXERCISE THREE

FROM IDEALISING TO REALISING YOUR PARTNER

This exercise helps you and your fiancé gently move from any idealized picture you may have of each other to seeing the real person God has made. Under the New Covenant, neither of you has to be perfect or live up to an ideal image to be fully loved and accepted. Christ has already made you both complete and righteous in Him.

The goal here is not to score each other or prove you're "good enough." It's to celebrate the real person God created and to let grace deepen your love as you see each other more clearly. Grace covers every gap between the "ideal" and the "real." Rest in Christ's perfect love for both of you, and let that love help you accept and cherish the real person in front of you.

Instructions

On your own first, rate how much each trait describes you and how much you think it describes your fiancé. Use this scale:

1 = Not at all
2 = A little
3 = Somewhat
4 = Mostly
5 = Very much

Your ranking of you		Your ranking of your Partner		Your Partner's actual ranking		Difference
________	Compassionate	________	-	________	=	________
________	Patient	________	-	________	=	________
________	Secure	________	-	________	=	________
________	Nurturing	________	-	________	=	________
________	Insightful	________	-	________	=	________
________	Confident	________	-	________	=	________
________	Relaxed	________	-	________	=	________
________	Tender	________	-	________	=	________
________	Even Tempered	________	-	________	=	________
________	Honest	________	-	________	=	________
________	Healthy	________	-	________	=	________
________	Spiritual	________	-	________	=	________
________	Consistent	________	-	________	=	________

Next steps

Share your ratings openly with each other. Write your partner's actual self-ratings in the third column (you can add this column to your sheet).

For each trait, calculate the difference (your ranking of them minus their self-ranking). Note any big gaps (e.g., difference of 2 or more).

Discuss gently:

- Where did you see each other more positively than they see themselves? Celebrate those places—thank God for the grace you see in each other!
- Where was there a gap? No blame. Simply share: "I saw you as more [trait] than you see yourself. What does [trait] look like for you in real life?"
- How does knowing you are already fully accepted and complete in Christ change the way you view these differences or "imperfections"?
- How can resting in His finished work help you love and accept the real person (not just the ideal image) every day?

Closing reflection

One of the most beautiful gifts of early marriage is moving from "idealizing" to "realizing" your partner. Grace makes this safe: because Christ already sees and loves the real you—flaws, growth areas, and all—you can offer the same grace to each other. You don't have to be perfect, to be loved. You are already loved perfectly in Christ. As you rest in that truth, the Holy Spirit produces genuine acceptance, patience, and tenderness (Galatians 5:22–23), so your love becomes deeper and more real, not based on an ideal, but on the real person God gave you.

Prayer (short and simple)

"Lord Jesus, thank You that You love and accept the real us—every part. Help us rest in Your finished work so we can see and cherish the real person You gave us. Let Your grace cover every gap and make our love deeper and truer. Amen."

EXERCISE FOUR

EXPLORING UNFINISHED BUSINESS

Marriage is not a quick fix for avoiding your own personal problems. In fact, marriage may even intensify those problems. Spend some time with the Holy Spirit, assessing if there are any expectations or needs that you are bringing into the marriage that your partner cannot fulfil. Write these down.

When we marry, we long to recreate the love and closeness and nurturance that we experienced or wish we had experienced in our relationship with our parents. But marriage is not always the place for those yearnings to be fulfilled. No human can meet another person's every need; deep relational longings are ultimately met only in a relationship with God.

If you are willing, share your writing with your partner and discuss the baggage you are both bringing into your marriage.

EXERCISE FIVE

RESTING IN YOUR IDENTITY IN CHRIST

This exercise invites honest reflection on how deeply you are resting in who God declares you to be through the Finished Work of the Cross. In the New Covenant, you are already fully loved, accepted, righteous, and complete in Christ (Colossians 2:10; Ephesians 1:6). Your worth isn't earned or improved by performance—it's a gift received by faith.

When we root our security in Christ's unchanging love rather than our own feelings or achievements, we enter marriage free to give and receive love without demands or fear. "We love because He first loved us" (1 John 4:19). Use this not as a "self-esteem test" to score or fix yourself, but as a prompt to affirm God's truth over any lies of unworthiness, and to discuss how this foundation strengthens your future marriage.

Answer each statement with one of these:

- **Yes—by God's grace, I rest in this truth**
- **Usually—I'm growing in resting here**
- **Seldom—I need to renew my mind more in God's Word**
- **No—I'm struggling and would value prayer/support**

	Yes	Usually	Seldom	No
Do you stand confidently on biblical values and truths rooted in Christ's finished work, even when others disagree, because your acceptance comes from Him?	o	o	o	o
Do you act on decisions guided by Scripture and the leading of the Holy Spirit, resting in your righteousness in Christ, without being crushed by others' disapproval?	o	o	o	o
Do you release worries about tomorrow and past mistakes to God, trusting His grace and forgiveness through the cross, knowing He works all things for good?	o	o	o	o
Do you have confidence that Christ in you is sufficient to handle challenges and setbacks, because His strength is made perfect in weakness?	o	o	o	o
Do you see yourself as equal in value to others—not superior or inferior—because God loves you fully in Christ and shows no favoritism?	o	o	o	o
Do you rest in the truth that you are deeply valued and delighted in by God, so you can receive interest and care from others without desperation?	o	o	o	o
Do you receive genuine praise or compliments humbly, without pride or guilt, knowing any good in you is from Christ's life in you?	o	o	o	o

	Yes	Usually	Seldom	No
Do you stand firm in your God-given identity and boundaries in Christ, resisting unhealthy control or domination while honoring others in grace?	o	o	o	o
Do you honestly acknowledge your full range of emotions (anger, love, sadness, joy, etc.) without shame, knowing you are forgiven and empowered by grace to respond in ways that honor Christ?	o	o	o	o
Do you enjoy life and various activities with freedom and gratitude, resting in the joy Christ gives, rather than needing constant achievement or approval to feel worthwhile?	o	o	o	o
Do you naturally sense and respond to others' needs with compassion, flowing from the love Christ has poured into your heart by the Holy Spirit?	o	o	o	o

- Which statements feel strongest because of what Jesus has already done in you? Thank God for that grace!
- Where do you sense the need to more fully believe and rest in your identity in Christ? How might Scripture, prayer, or your fiancé encourage you here?
- How does resting in Christ's completeness change the way you will love and be loved in marriage—without needing your spouse to "fix" or complete you?

IMPORTANT ISSUES

1. With your partner, discuss the expectations you have of your life together. What unspoken values or expectations do each of you bring into your partnership? In what ways might they influence the quality of your marriage?

____

____

____

____

____

____

____

____

____

2. What three important things have you already given up (or are you willing to give up) as you prepare for marriage? Have you honestly acknowledged and brought those changes/losses to the Lord in prayer? What greater joys or freedoms do you anticipate gaining in Christ-centered marriage as a result?

3. In dating, how have you both (intentionally or unintentionally) presented a "best version" to impress or attract? How can resting in Christ's unconditional acceptance free you to be fully authentic with each other now and in marriage, allowing grace to deepen genuine intimacy?

4. How does receiving God's unconditional love and acceptance through Christ's finished work empower you to love your spouse freely? In what ways might resting in your identity in Him (fully loved and complete—Col. 2:10) change how you give and receive love in marriage?

5. How does Christ's finished work provide the true healing and wholeness we need (Isaiah 53:5; Col. 2:10)? In what areas do you sense the need for deeper renewal by the Holy Spirit?

6. How does being complete and secure in Christ (Col. 2:10) free you from unhealthy dependency or isolated independence? What does grace-empowered interdependence look like—two heirs together of the grace of life (1 Peter 3:7) choosing to support and grow in Christ?

7. Honestly list your reasons for wanting to marry. How many reflect resting in God's provision and calling versus seeking completion, security, or healing that only Christ provides? Pray together: Is this a God-led choice rooted in His grace?

8. Prayerfully make notes on what draws you to your partner and any areas that need growth in the relationship. How does seeing each other through the lens of grace (as beloved in Christ) shift your perspective from pros/cons to celebrating God's workmanship (Eph. 2:10) and trusting Him for transformation?

9. What role has God played in bringing you together? Have you sought Him in prayer, both individually and as a couple? Do you sense this is a "God choice" led by His grace and peace, rather than just a good human decision?

---

10. Do you know and trust each other's personal history? How has your partner shown growth in past relationships? How do you see Christ's grace at work in each other's lives and in your relationship now?

---

11. Why do you believe God is leading you into marriage at this time? How are you resting in His grace to equip you for covenant partnership?

____

12. In what ways does your relationship reveal areas where Christ's transforming grace is at work in you? How can you encourage each other to rest more fully in Him so His best shines through?

13. Does your relationship draw you both closer to Christ and deeper into His grace? Are you growing together as heirs of the grace of life (1 Peter 3:7), passionate about pursuing God?

14. How might your work/career affect your marriage?

15. What shared goals do you have for your marriage and life together? Be specific (3 months, 6 months, 1 year, 5 years.) How will you depend on God's grace and leading to pursue them, rather than self-effort?

Shared Goals for Marriage	
3 months:	
6 months:	
1 year:	
5 years:	

16. What potential obstacles might arise? How can resting in Christ's sufficiency and praying together as heirs of grace help overcome them?

17. How do you view seeking Godly counsel or marriage mentoring? Are you open to grace-based guidance that points you to Christ's Finished Work?

18. How do you plan to grow spiritually together—through prayer, Scripture, worship?

____

____

____

____

____

____

19. How well do you know your partner? Knowing your partner deeply reflects the intimacy Christ has with His church. Use this to celebrate grace at work and identify areas to pursue understanding under His love.

		True	**False**
1.	I can name my partner's 3 best friends	o	o
2.	I know what accomplishments my partner is most proud of.	o	o
3.	I can identify the happiest time in my partner's life	o	o
4.	I know what my partner considers to be his/her greatest area of difficulty in interacting with each parent.	o	o
5.	I can describe what my partner considers to be his/her greatest losses in life.	o	o
6.	I know what radio station my partner will be tuned into / music he/she will listen to when driving somewhere	o	o
7.	I can name the relatives that my partner would most likely try to avoid	o	o
8.	I can describe the most traumatic event that occurred in my partner's childhood.	o	o
9.	My partner has clearly identified for me what he/she wants in life.	o	o
10.	I can identify the obstacles that my partner believes are standing in his/her way of what he/she wants	o	o

		True	False
11.	I know which of my partner's physical features he/she is the least happy with	o	o
12.	I can recall the first impression I had of my partner.	o	o
13.	I can describe, in some detail, the home environment my partner was raised in.	o	o
14.	I know what makes my partner laugh.	o	o
15.	I know which App my partner will access first when looking at his/her social media.	o	o
16.	I can name 2 or 3 decisions my partner made before we met that he/she regrets – and my partner can do the same about me.	o	o
17.	I know what my partner's parents would probably say is the thing about him/her they are the proudest of.	o	o
18.	I know which part of the restaurant menu my partner is likely to look at first.	o	o
19.	I know there are things my partner says to me that he/she says to no-one else in the world.	o	o
20.	I am thoroughly familiar with my partner's personal relationship with Christ and how the Finished Work of the Cross shapes their daily life and faith.	o	o
	Score		

For each True – 1 and each False – 0.

0 – 10: A score of 10 or less suggest that the opportunity to create an in-depth profile of your partner may be coming at a critical time in your relationship.

11-20: If you score higher than 10, it's fair to say that you've developed a pretty accurate profile of your partner. However, there's a great deal of exploration and discovery yet to come.

Whatever your score, there can be no more special feeling any of us has that to be focused on by our partner. The knowledge that our partner understands and appreciates our unique needs brings a special strength to the relationship.

Building Love that Endures

What on earth is this love that upsets everybody, and how is it to be distinguished from insanity?

W.S. Gilbert

Defining Love

When asked what makes a good marriage, ninety percent of people answer, "Being in love." Yet when asked what love actually is, the answers vary as widely as the people themselves. Some compare love to lighting. You may not know what it is, but you know when it hits you. Others say it is the feeling you feel when you have a feeling you've never felt before.

Under the New Covenant, true love flows from God's love for us in Christ. "We love because He first loved us" (1 John 4:19). As we rest in His finished work—fully accepted and complete in Him (Ephesians 1:6; Colossians 2:10)—the Holy Spirit empowers us to love our spouse freely. We love not to earn or maintain anything, but because love is who we are in Christ.

True love is not defined by feelings that come and go, but by the *agape* love God pours into our hearts through the Holy Spirit (Romans 5:5). God's kind of love is a decision we make based on Scripture and then act on in faith—feelings follow as we rest in Christ.

THE ANATOMY OF LOVE

Whatever love is, it is not easy to pin down, for love is a strange mixture of opposites. It includes excitement and boredom, stability and change, restriction and freedom. Love's ultimate paradox is two beings becoming one yet remaining two.

We as Christians have experienced the perfect love of our Heavenly Father, and from this we have begun to learn the nature of true love—as we look at the love that sent Jesus into this world and the love Jesus showed us when He died on the cross.

The Bible calls love a fruit of the Spirit, which results from the work of the Holy Spirit in our hearts when we allow Him to have His perfect way with us. Paul says that God is love. This does not mean God is an abstraction, but that as to His nature God is love and that love flows out of Him as a source. Since all love proceeds out of God as a source, all love must eventually be conformed to God's love if it is true.

In 1 Corinthians 13:7 (TLB) we read: "If you love someone, you will be loyal to him no matter what the cost. You will always believe in him, always expect the best of him, and always stand your ground in defending him." The attitudes brought out in this verse can be summed up in three words: loyalty, trust, and respect.

Love is built upon this tripod of loyalty, respect, and trust. Unless the foundation is acknowledged and lived out by grace, the whole structure remains shaky.

A. Triangular Model Of Love

It is important to take note of research done by Dr. Robert Sternberg. He developed the triangular model of love. In this model, love has 3 sides: passion, intimacy and commitment.

While models like Sternberg's describe human love, under the New Covenant the Holy Spirit produces a balanced love as we rest in Christ's perfect commitment to us (Hebrews 13:5). Passion, intimacy, and commitment flourish not by striving, but as grace teaches us how to live (Titus 2:11–12).

Passion

The motivational side of the triangle is passion—the spine-tingling sensation that moves us toward romance. Passion is sensual and sexual, characterized by physiological arousal and an intense desire for physical affection. The Song of Songs celebrates the physical love between a man and a woman in passion-filled poetry.

But passion can also be possessive, fostering a fascination that borders on obsession. At first, couples experience a rapidly growing physical attraction, but after a while they incorporate the ecstasy of passion into the fuller picture of love. Pure passion is self-seeking until it is linked with intimacy.

Intimacy

The emotional side of love's triangle is intimacy. Love without intimacy is only a hormonal illusion. One cannot desire another person over the long haul without really knowing that person.

Intimacy has a "best friend" or "soul mate" quality about it. We all have a need for someone to know us better than anyone else does—and still accept us. Intimacy fills our heart's deepest longings for closeness and acceptance.

People who have successfully built an intimate relationship know its power and comfort, but they also know that taking the emotional risk that allows intimacy to happen isn't easy. Without careful nurturing, intimacy withers.

Neil Clark Warren identifies lack of intimacy as the biggest enemy of marriage. Without intimacy, two people can never fully merge or bond and become "one flesh." They will be isolated and alone—even while living under the same roof.

The fulfillment of love hinges on closeness, sharing, communication, honesty, appreciation, consideration, and support. As one heart given in exchange for another, marriage provides the deepest and most radical expression of intimacy.

Commitment

The cognitive and willful side of the love triangle is commitment. Commitment creates a small island of certainty in the swirling waters of uncertainty. As the anchor of marriage, commitment secures love for our partner when passion burns low and when turbulent times and fierce impulses overtake us.

Commitment says, "I love you because you are you, not because of what you do or how I feel." The duration of love and the health of a marriage depend mightily on the strength of commitment—both to your partner and, most importantly, to God.

William Doherty describes two kinds of commitment. One is "commitment-as-long-as"—staying together only as long as things are working out for me. The other is "commitment-no-matter-what"—the long view of marriage in which you don't balance the ledgers every month to see if you are getting an adequate return on your investment. You're here to stay.

This "no-matter-what" commitment flows from resting in the New Covenant: Christ never leaves us, so we reflect His faithfulness by grace. It mirrors Christ's unbreakable love for His bride, sealed by His blood, not our performance.

Intentionality means making your marriage a high priority. During courtship the relationship is front and center. After marriage, other things often take priority. An intentional marriage means being conscious about maintaining connection through a reservoir of marital rituals of connection and intimacy.

We prioritize connection because we are already secure in Christ's love, freeing us to serve without scorekeeping.

The main way to resist the forces that pull us apart—the neutral drift of marriage over time and the insidious pull of consumer culture—is to be a couple who carefully cultivates commitment and ways to connect over the years. The intentional couple thinks about their relationship, plans for their relationship, and acts for their relationship, mostly in simple, everyday ways and occasionally in big, splashy ways.

HOW IS LOVE GIVEN AND RECEIVED?

To answer this question, we need to study love styles and love's stages.

1. Love Styles

It is wrong to assume that love means to our partners what it means to us. The way you give love may not be the way your partner wants to be loved. This can cause a lot of hurt and confusion. It is important to be aware of your partner's love style so you can adapt to it.

Using Dr. Sternberg's triangle, a triangle with three equal sides represents consummate love, in which all three components are equally matched. This is ideal, but when one leg becomes longer than the others, an unbalanced kind of love style emerges: romantic, foolish, or companionable.

- Romantic love relies on intimacy and passion, with commitment taking a back seat.
- Foolish love results from passion and commitment without the stabilizing element of intimate knowledge.
- Companionable love evolves from intimacy and commitment, with passion fading into the background (remember the dangers of the companionate marriage in Session 1?).

Successful marriages demand more than any of these unbalanced styles. Consummate love is not achieved by perfect balance through effort—it is the fruit of resting in Christ's love, allowing the Spirit to grow passion, intimacy, and commitment in us over time.

Since we are loved perfectly by Christ, we can choose to express love in ways that fill our spouse's heart—not to earn their love, but to reflect the unconditional love we've received. The Holy Spirit empowers us to speak these languages with genuine grace.

2. Love's Languages

Love languages help us understand how to express the agape we've received, no manipulation, just reflecting Christ's love freely. (This is just a brief overview of the Book: The 5 Love Languages by Gary Chapman)

Language 1: Words of Affirmation

Marriages can be destroyed or built on words. We speak life because Christ speaks life over us. Compliments, encouragement, appreciation, kind words, and humble requests (not demands) all build up. Love makes requests, not demands. Requests affirm worth and ability.

Language 2: Quality Time

Quality time is giving your partner your undivided attention. It includes togetherness, meaningful conversation, learning to talk (self-revelation), and quality activities. The essential ingredients are that at least one wants to do it, the other is willing, and both know why—to express love by being together. Quality activities make memories

Language 3: Receiving Gifts

A gift is a symbol that someone thought of you. It doesn't have to be expensive; it is the thought that counts. Visual symbols of love are more important to some people than to others. Being there when your partner needs you is also a powerful gift of self.

Language 4: Acts of Service

Acts of service mean doing things you know your partner would like you to do. Jesus served from fullness, not lack—He washed feet knowing His identity (John 13:3-5). We serve our spouse the same way, resting in who we already are in Christ.

Language 5: Physical Touch

Physical touch is a powerful way of communicating love. It can make or break a marriage. Partners who have touch as a primary love language don't always want it to lead to sex. Meeting your partner's need for love is a choice you make every day. If you know your partner's primary love language and choose to speak it, their deepest emotional need will be met, and they will feel secure in your love.

A. Love's Stages

Love changes over time, but under grace it deepens into something richer and more beautiful. As the initial rush of romance naturally fades, Christ's unchanging love anchors us. The Holy Spirit then produces deeper intimacy, care, and creativity. These stages are not achievements we must strive for or boxes we must check. They are seasons in which grace transforms us from glory to glory (2 Corinthians 3:18). The word glory means view, opinion or outlook. The power struggle reveals our need to die to self-effort and rest in Christ's sufficiency. Co-creativity overflows as we live as heirs together of the grace of life (1 Peter 3:7).

Every marriage faces predictable passages that test and strengthen a couple's bond: adjusting to each other, launching careers, the birth of children, children leaving home, serious illness, and retirement. If change is not expected, love can be thrown off course. But when a marriage is rooted in grace and change is anticipated, love finds new depths of fulfillment.

Here are the five sequential seasons of love in marriage. Each one builds on the one before it and offers fresh opportunities to rest in Christ and let His life flow through your relationship.

Stage 1: Romance

The first stage of marriage is romance—a time of enchantment when couples often forget they are still two unique individuals. In this season of delight, the couple takes complete joy in each other. They reach for their deepest needs for intimacy and experience a kind of mystical union. They celebrate the ecstasy of belonging.

Under grace, this stage is a wonderful gift, but it is not the foundation. The real foundation is Christ's perfect love. As the initial intensity softens, couples are invited to move from idealizing each other to resting in the One who already loves them perfectly (Ephesians 1:6). Romance becomes sweeter when it flows from fullness rather than need.

Stage 2: Power Struggle

This stage begins when individuality, habits, and differences emerge and become glaring. Two independent people forming a life together inevitably run into power struggles and must learn to adjust to each other's ways. The intensity varies, but almost every couple experiences it.

Successful passage through this stage enables each partner to say, "Okay, I am willing to admit that my romance with a perfect partner was an illusion. However, I am still fascinated with the mystery of who you are, and I am willing to pursue a more mature love with you."

Under grace, the power struggle is not a sign that something is wrong with the marriage. It is an opportunity to die to self-effort and rest in Christ's sufficiency. Here we learn that we cannot change our spouse through striving, but the Holy Spirit can transform both of us as we behold Jesus (2 Corinthians 3:18). This stage teaches us to stop demanding that our partner meet needs that only Christ can fill.

Stage 3: Co-operation

This stage feels like a breath of fresh air for couples who have stayed the course through the power struggle. A new sense of acceptance and willingness to change enters the relationship. Couples realize that love is not so much looking outward at each other but looking inward at themselves and taking responsibility for their own issues.

They give up the illusion that their partner is supposed to make them happy and begin redefining love by facing their own fears, defenses, projections, and hurts.

Under grace, cooperation becomes natural. Because we are already loved and accepted in Christ, we no longer need our spouse to complete us. We can serve, forgive, and adjust from fullness rather than lack. The Holy Spirit produces the patience and humility needed for true teamwork.

Stage 4: Mutuality

Mutuality is a season of feeling at one with each other, where each partner experiences a secure sense of belonging. Just as couples wonder if they will ever escape old unhealthy patterns, they discover a new reality and are surprised by the joy of mutual intimacy.

Under grace, this stage reveals the beauty of two people who are secure in Christ choosing to be "us" without losing their individuality. It is a foretaste of the oneness God designed—two hearts beating in rhythm because both are resting in the same love that never fails.

Stage 5: Co-creativity

In this mature stage, the intimacy each couple yearns for becomes a lived reality. As partners grow older, retire, and face the end of life together, they develop a pronounced energy of creativity. Intimacy comes to a new and final flourish, and love overflows. Secure in themselves and in their love, couples develop a web of meaningful interrelationships that support the marriage and deepen its joys.

Although love changes over a lifetime, it becomes no less intimate, no less meaningful, and no less important. As young passion recedes, it is replaced with a deeper, more abiding sense of intimacy, care, and co-creativity. The flame may burn lower, but the coals glow warmer and longer.

Couples in this stage reflect Christ's love to the world, living as heirs together of the grace of life (1 Peter 3:7). Their marriage becomes a quiet testimony that lasting oneness is not the result of human effort, but the fruit of resting in the Finished Work of Jesus.

MAKING LOVE LAST A LIFETIME

Lifelong love does not happen by chance or human mastery alone. It flows from resting in Christ's finished work. As we abide in Him, His love sustains our marriage through every season (John 15:9). We cultivate passion, intimacy, and commitment not by striving, but by depending on the grace that teaches us to say "No" to ungodliness and to live self-controlled, upright, and godly lives (Titus 2:11–12).

Every successful marriage is the result of two people working tirelessly and skillfully to cultivate their love. When they combine passion, intimacy and commitment, they are able to grow a flourishing, healthy marriage.

1. Cultivate Passion

The loss of passionate romance in marriage is a common complaint, whether couples have been married one or twenty-five years. It is unrealistic to expect the exhilarating peaks of passion to remain constant, but marriage in no way requires passion to be put on ice. How does one rekindle the sometimes-flickering flame of passion?

Practice meaningful touch. Affection in the form of touching is not only a preliminary to making love; it is a language that speaks more eloquently than words.

Plan mutually enjoyable experiences. Being married doesn't mean the fun has to end. Successful couples work diligently to associate their partners with positive experiences. Passion can only survive and thrive if the couple continue "dating" even after they marry.

Compliment your partner daily. The most important element of romantic passion for both husbands and wives are to feel special. They want to know that they are appreciated. Compliments feel good, both to give and receive.

Resting in Christ's delight over us frees us to enjoy each other.

2. Cultivate Intimacy

Ideally, husbands and wives are best friends as well as lovers, sharing dreams, interests, fears and hopes. Unconditional acceptance mirrors how Christ accepts us fully.

The gap between true intimacy and real life remains wide. To cultivate intimacy in marriage:

Spend time together: One of the greatest illusions is that love is self-sustaining. Love must be fed and nurtured and this demands time. Studies have shown that happiness is highly correlated with the amount of time spent together. Make time for each other!

Listen with a third ear. Studies on intimate sharing indicate that not really listening is the most fundamental error couples make. We have a tendency to interrupt or be impatient while our partner is telling a story. Intimacy is cultivated when we patiently listen – not only to the story, but also to the feelings our partner is conveying. If you learn that simple skill, intimacy will blossom in your marriage.

Practice unconditional acceptance. The deepest kind of sharing can only take place when there is no fear of rejection. Nothing drains a relationship of intimacy faster than anxiety and nothing promotes intimacy more than knowing you are unconditionally accepted, even though you aren't perfect.

Focus on commonalities. Intimacy grows when nurtured by shared emotions, experiences and beliefs. Any couple, who have been happily married for fifty years, will tell you their differences, but in spite of the differences you will hear commonalities. The more couples focus on what they have in common, the deeper intimacy grows.

Explore spiritual terrain together. A lack of intimacy can often be traced to a lack of spiritual vitality. When two people have a spiritual hunger or spiritual awareness in common, they become soul mates. In other words–spirituality is the soul of marriage. Without spiritual roots, couples are left with an emptiness and superficiality that prevent genuine intimacy. Partners who do not cultivate intimacy in their marriage will live in an emotional and spiritual vacuum, never enjoying the full beauty of love.

3. Cultivate Commitment

While the rush of romantic feelings will eventually fade, another kind of love, anchored in commitment, will take place and bring stability and peace to your marriage.

Assess the high value of commitment. Three doctors who studied 6000 marriages and 3000 divorces, concluded: "There may be nothing more important in the marriage than a determination that it will persist. With such determination individuals force themselves to adjust and to accept situations which would seem sufficient grounds for a break-up, if continuation of the marriage were not the prime objective." Commitment is the cement that holds the stones of marriage in place.

Meet your partner's needs. Human beings have a fundamental need for security. One of the best ways to give people security is to meet their day-to-day needs. Once partners meet each other's need to unwind after work, or have one night out a week, for example, the level of security in the relationship rises. Meeting even the smallest of needs can cultivate the security of commitment.

Honor your partner's promise. People can become so focused on their own commitment and sacrifices they are making for their marriage that they miss the importance of their partner's promise to them.

Make your commitment part of your being. As human beings, we create and define ourselves through commitments and those commitments become an integral part of our identity. When we contradict our commitments, we lose ourselves and suffer an identity crisis. You can strengthen your commitment to your partner by choosing to make it a vital part of your being, by giving it top priority, so much so that to break it is to break who you are. Commitment rests on Christ's 'I will never leave you' (Heb. 13:5).

Once again, every marriage is grounded in passion, intimacy, and commitment. Cultivating these three elements will help you successfully navigate the stages of love and make it last a lifetime. We don't strive to rekindle by human skill alone: passion flows from resting in Christ's delight over us (Zephaniah 3:17).

FOOD FOR THOUGHT

Love is that condition in which the happiness of another person is essential to your own.

God's kind of love is not based on feelings; it is a choice to act on what God says about loving your spouse—even when emotions lag. As you rest in the finished work, the Holy Spirit will produce this love in you.

EXERCISE 1

DEFINING LOVE

This exercise will help you define love in your own terms and compare your definition with your partners. Through a study done by researcher Beverly Fear, the following twelve attributes had been identified as the most central features of love. Take a moment and prioritize this list for yourself (with the most important as #1). This is not a performance test.

_______ acceptance

_______ caring

_______ commitment

_______ concern for the other's well-being

_______ friendship

_______ honesty

_______ interest in others

_______ loyalty

_______ respect

_______ supportiveness

_______ trust

_______ wanting to be with each other

Next, circle your top three attributes of love and write a definition of love that incorporates them.

Love is:

____

____

____

____

____

____

____

Now compare your priorities and your definition with your fiancé to see what differences, if any, you might have when it comes to defining love.

EXERCISE 2

CULTIVATING INTIMACY

This exercise will help you open your heart and increase your level of intimacy. Begin by writing about your shared experiences. What is it about each other's background that draws you together? What things set the two of you apart from others? What experiences have you had together that bring back fond memories. And how does resting in Christ's love help you share fears/hopes more openly?

EXERCISE 3

Next, focus on things that the two of you share. Begin by jotting down one or two things in each of the following categories, then discuss them with your fiancé. The more detailed you can be, the better.

1. Interests we have in common include:

2. Plans we share for our future include:

3. Fears and anxieties we both have include:

4. Hopes and dreams we share include:

5. Spiritual beliefs we both have include:

____

____

____

____

Conclude this exercise by talking in specific terms about what the two of you can do to cultivate more emotional intimacy in your relationship.

EXERCISE 4

Please read 1 Corinthians 13:1-13 using a modern translation. On a scale from 1-10 assess yourself as well as your partner on the aspects of love. 10 being highest and 1 the lowest.

Use it to celebrate where grace is already at work and to see where you may need to receive more of His transforming love and power.

	SELF	PARTNER
PATIENT		
KIND		
ENVY		
BOAST		
PROUD		
RUDE		
SELF-SEEKING		
ANGER		
WRONGS		
EVIL		
TRUTH		

Referring back to the notes, also rate yourself on:

	SELF	PARTNER
LOYALTY		
TRUST		
RESPECT		

Where you scored lower, how might receiving more of God's grace (Titus 2:11-12) and renewing your mind to who you are in Christ help the Holy Spirit grow that aspect of love in your relationship? Pray together about one area and ask God to empower you by grace."

MARRIAGE CHECK LIST

We pledge to love each other with the principles of the Bible being our guide:

From 1 Corinthians 13:4-7

LOVE IS PATIENT Are we patient with each other? Do we bear with one another's weaknesses?

LOVE IS KIND Are we treating each other with loving kindness – and grace? Are we tender-hearted in our attitudes – and our actions? Are we being cynical and critical? Are we using cutting humor in how we relate to one another?

IT DOES NOT ENVY Has a spirit of envy been displayed by either one of us? Are we exhibiting discontentment or resentment in what we have or don't have?

IT DOES NOT BOAST; IT IS NOT PROUD Are we being boastful, arrogant, or haughty? Are we displaying an attitude of being more superior or smarter than the other?

IT IS NOT RUDE. Are we being rude, intolerant, or harsh with each other?

IT IS NOT SELF-SEEKING. Are we living together in partnership – not allowing our individual wants to take precedence over our relationship as a marital team? Are we giving back or only taking?

IT IS NOT EASILY ANGERED. Are we being too irritable or hyper-sensitive

IT KEEPS NO RECORD OF WRONGS. Are we being too "historical" with each other? Are we keeping score of that which we shouldn't?

LOVE DOES NOT DELIGHT IN EVIL BUT REJOICES WITH THE TRUTH? Are we amusing ourselves with that which would not please God? Are we taking delight in that which we shouldn't? When we converse, are we speaking the truth in love?

IT ALWAYS PROTECTS. Are we protecting each other's feelings? Do we rudely embarrass or belittle each other? Can it be interpreted in any way that we are attacking each other's character?

ALWAYS TRUSTS. Are we living lives of trustworthiness? Are we putting our trust in Christ? Do we believe the best of our spouse?

ALWAYS HOPES. Are there times when we're being too quick to assume the worst in each other? Do we have hope because of Christ?

ALWAYS PERSEVERES. Are we giving up too easily? Are we persevering through problems and conflicts rather than caving into them?

EXERCISE 5

1. When did you first say, "I love you" to your partner? Recount the experience. What were your thoughts and feelings?

____

____

____

____

____

____

2. Which component of love seems most powerful in your relationship at the moment: Passion, commitment or intimacy? Why?

____

____

____

____

____

____

3. What do you do in your relationship to cultivate intimacy – especially when you are busy?

____

____

____

____

____

____

4. Passion is typically the first component of love to fade in marriage. What can you do to prepare for this and prevent passion from dying completely?

____

____

____

5. How has your concept of love changed as a result of reading this chapter? Can you list some specific things you can do to make love a lifetime?

____

____

____

6. What does commitment mean to you?

____

____

____

7. Are there situations where you would consider being entitled to break your commitment to your partner? Why?

____

____

____

8. How do you plan to keep your marriage intentional?

____

____

____

Celebrate the areas where grace has already grown you and pray together over any areas that still need renewal in Christ.

A DEFINITION OF LOVE by Chuck Swindoll

Little children, let us not love with word or with tongue, but in deed and truth." 1 John 3:18

L – LISTEN: When we love others, we respect and accept them enough to graciously listen to what they say and feel.

O – OVERLOOK: For most of us, the first thing we notice in others is their flaws. Accepting others in love, however, entails passing over their weaknesses so that we can affirm their strengths.

V – VALUE: How often do we say we love someone yet make them feel inferior through put downs and harsh words. Real love honors and esteems others, making them feel valuable and capable.

E – EXPRESS: Love is a verb – it acts, it gives, it demonstrates itself in tangible ways.

The Greek writer Aristedes once described to the Emperor Hadrian how the early Christians expressed their love: "They love one another. They never fail to help the widows; they save orphans from those who would hurt them. If they have something they give freely to the man who has nothing; If they have something they give freely to the man who has nothing; if they see a stranger, they take him home and are happy, as though he were a real brother. They don't consider themselves brothers in the usual sense but brothers instead through the Spirit, in God."

Attitude with Latitude!

Happiness has no reason. It is not found in the facts of our lives, but in the color of the light by which we look at the facts. True joy isn't circumstantial: it is the fruit of resting in Christ's unchanging love!

Consider The Magnitude Of Your Attitude

It is no accident that some couples navigate marital turbulence successfully while others in similar circumstances are tossed by frustration, disappointment, and eventual despair.

Happiness in marriage is not found in perfect circumstances, but in the light of God's grace through Christ's finished work. Some couples thrive because they rest in Christ's unchanging love and allow the Holy Spirit to renew their minds (Romans 12:2). True joy is a fruit of the Spirit (Galatians 5:22), produced as we abide in Jesus and choose to focus on His truth rather than our changing situations.

WHAT EXACTLY IS AN ATTITUDE?

Simply put, an attitude is a feeling inside that we display by the way we behave.

"As a man thinks in his heart, so is he" (Proverbs 23:7, NKJV).

In the New Covenant, we are responsible for our attitude, yet we do not strive to manufacture one in our own strength. God calls us to have the same attitude as Christ Jesus (Philippians 2:5), and He Himself works in us "both to will and to work for His good pleasure" (Philippians 2:13). Grace empowers the change as we rest in who we already are in Him.

PROGRAMMING OUR MIND FOR A HAPPY MARRIAGE

Not all of us start married life with an abundance of material goods and in the beginning, it seems of little importance that you don't own a house or that money is in short supply because you haven't been able to get a better paying job. However, there might come a time when we become dissatisfied with our circumstances, especially when we look at other couples who seem to have everything.

Under grace, we renew our minds by beholding Christ (2 Corinthians 3:18). When circumstances feel discouraging, we do not try to force positivity. Instead, we turn to God's truth: we are already loved, accepted, and complete in Christ (Colossians 2:10; Ephesians 1:6). As we fix our eyes on Jesus, the Holy Spirit produces His joy and peace in us (Romans 14:17).

Renewing the mind isn't positive thinking: it's beholding Jesus until we see ourselves as He sees us: complete and accepted (Ephesians 1:6). This shifts perspective so the Holy Spirit produces joy and peace (Romans 14:17)."

THE POWER OF NEGATIVE THINKING

Most negative people feel they could be positive if only they had a different job, lived in a better place, or were married to a different person. The truth is that happiness does not hinge on better circumstances. A bad attitude does not change simply because circumstances do.

By force of habit, each of us is either basically positive or basically negative. Consider David and Goliath: While the Israelites looked at the giant and thought, "He is so big, we can never kill him," David looked at him and said, "He is so big, I can never miss him!" David saw God's power, not the giant's size. His confidence came from faith in God's sufficiency, not from positive thinking. In marriage, we look to Christ's sufficiency (Philippians 4:13) rather than our spouse's flaws.

Negative interpretations are guaranteed to bleed the happiness out of marriage. The good news is that we can take responsibility for our own feelings and interpretations. Dr. Victor Frankl, while suffering in a Nazi concentration camp, realized that no one could take away his freedom to choose how he would react. In Christ we have even greater power—the Holy Spirit renews us (Ephesians 4:23) and gives strength (Philippians 4:13).

Negativity always distorts the truth, limits God, limits others, limits our enjoyment of life, and is contagious. But when we recognize that the control lies in ourselves and not in external events, we are able to interpret upsetting situations differently and develop a positive attitude by grace.

THE SECRET OF HAPPY COUPLES

Without the capacity to rise above circumstances, you will never cultivate lasting happiness. Every happy couple has learned to cultivate the right attitude in spite of the circumstances they find themselves in. Paul said, "I have learned in whatever state I am, to be content" (Philippians 4:11).

The road to happiness is always under construction. The happiest people don't necessarily have the best of everything. They just make the best of everything they have. The happiest couples rest in Christ's contentment, making the best of what God provides as heirs together of the grace of life (1 Peter 3:7).

The secret is resting in Christ's contentment (Philippians 4:11–13 — "I can do all things through Christ who strengthens me"). We do not rely on externals or self-mastery; we abide in Jesus, where joy is full (John 15:11). Living happily ever after becomes reality as grace transforms our attitudes, helping us make the best of what God provides.

SABOTEURS OF HAPPINESS IN MARRIAGE

It's not always the big things that sabotage a marriage. Often, it's the accumulation of little things that are never dealt with while they are still small. These small issues can build up and eventually cause a painful blow-up.

Little things can slip in that seem insignificant at the time. But if we are not paying attention, they can cause disproportionate damage to something as valuable as our marriage.

Song of Solomon 2:15 (CJB) says: "Catch the foxes for us, yes, the little foxes! They are ruining the vineyards when our vineyards are in bloom!"

This verse uses little foxes as a picture of small, seemingly harmless issues that can destroy something beautiful. The vineyards in bloom represent a season of growth, beauty, and great potential — which is exactly what a new marriage is! That's why it is so important to protect it.

The call to "catch the foxes" is an invitation to proactive vigilance. It encourages us to notice and remove even minor threats before they grow bigger. This principle applies to many areas of married life: unspoken resentments, small habits that annoy us, or even everyday things like leaving an empty roll of toilet paper on the holder.

1. **Self-Pity**

Self-pity is a luxury no happy marriage can afford. It bleeds the joy out of a relationship and hurts not only ourselves, but those around us. Tough times and bitter experiences are part of every couple's life, but self-pity only adds to the burden. Grace frees us from self-pity as we receive God's comfort (2 Corinthians 1:3–4) and choose gratitude instead.

2. **Naming and Blaming**

To err is human; to blame it on somebody else is even more human! Ever since Adam blamed Eve and Eve blamed the serpent (and the serpent didn't have a leg to stand on!), couples have used the trick of finding excuses and shifting responsibility. A great deal of unhappiness can be traced to a mate's habitual tendency to blame his or her spouse.

In many relationships one of the partners is a scapegoat. The other partner sees him and her as the source of their difficulties. In effect, the blaming partner is saying: "You are my problem". But he or she would have a hard time finding a marriage counsellor who agrees. Professionals know better. They know that marital unhappiness is never caused by only one person. That is why counsellors focus not on who is wrong, but on what is wrong. To err is human; to blame it on somebody else is even more human. Ever since Adam blamed Eve and Eve blamed the serpent, couples have shifted responsibility. A great deal of unhappiness can be traced to the habit of blaming one's spouse.

Blame blocks unity; grace empowers personal responsibility and quick forgiveness (Ephesians 4:32). If you are angry, it is not your spouse's fault but your own choice of response. The habit of blaming is completely contrary to taking responsibility for our own attitude.

3. **Resentment**

Resentment is like a cancer to a relationship. At first, small and unnoticed, it grows larger and spreads its poison through the entire marriage. When we dwell on injustice, replaying it over and over, it triggers more negative emotions and convinces us that our spouse is the source of our unhappiness.

Resentment, bitterness, and unforgiveness are among the most toxic emotions. Even when directed at someone other than our spouse, they harm the marriage and our walk with God. Unforgiveness hinders our own experience of God's grace. But as we rest in how much we have been forgiven (Ephesians 4:32), the Holy Spirit enables us to forgive freely—with no scorekeeping. Forgiveness is not merely an emotion; it is a choice empowered by grace. Jesus instructed us to forgive "seventy times seven" (Matthew 18:22). A happy marriage cannot survive the cancer of resentment, but when it is released, nothing stands in the way of living in the joy Christ has provided.

HAPPILY EVER AFTER – FACT OR FICTION

Every couple about to be married cherishes dreams of a "perfect" life together. No matter how ideally suited they are, every husband and wife eventually realize that theirs is not a perfect match. Merging two personalities, preferences, and backgrounds is much more difficult than anticipated.

Marriage isn't perfect because people aren't perfect—but Christ is. Resting in His finished work frees us from demanding perfection from our spouse and allows grace to cover every fault and weakness.

The habit of joy is an inside reality because Christ lives in us. As we renew our minds daily with God's truth (Romans 12:2) and submit our circumstances to Him, the Holy Spirit produces lasting joy and peace. "Happily ever after" becomes a grace-filled journey, not a fairy tale.

FOOD FOR THOUGHT

To live in love is life's greatest challenge. It requires more subtlety, flexibility, sensitivity, understanding, acceptance, tolerance, knowledge and strength than any other human endeavor or emotion. Leo Busgaglia

Love's greatest challenge is met not by human effort alone, but by the grace of God at work in us.

EXERCISE 1

This exercise helps you see how your thoughts shape your moods and your relationship. Under grace, our feelings often follow what we think (Proverbs 23:7), but lasting change comes as we renew our minds with God's truth (Romans 12:2; Philippians 4:8). As we rest in Christ's finished work, we invite the Holy Spirit to replace negative self-talk with His peace and joy.

1. List three circumstances that typically get you into a rotten mood. For example: being stuck in traffic, waiting for someone to arrive who is late, having your credit card rejected, and so on.

____

____

____

____

2. There is a maxim in psychology that says, "you feel what you think." In other words, your feelings are the result of what is going on in your mind. For each of the bad circumstances you listed above, write down what you are saying to yourself that makes you feel so rotten. For example: "I could be relaxing in front of the TV instead of waiting for this person who is always late."

____

____

____

3. Now, renew your thinking by turning to God's truth. Write three alternative statements rooted in Scripture or Christ's love that could bring peace instead of frustration. For example: 'This wait is annoying, but I can use it to pray and rest in God's timing (Psalm 37:7).

____

____

____

____

____

____

4. Negative self-talk also affects our response to more serious situations. To see how negative self-talk may have affected you, list two situations in your life that were difficult or painful to deal with. For example: "Losing a loved one or a job, breaking off a relationship, or going through serious illness."

---

5. For each of the crises you listed above, write down things you said to yourself that added to your pain. For example: "This relationship ended because I'm just such a loser."

---

6. For painful situations, reflect on negative self-talk that added hurt. Then, write alternative truths from God's Word that could have brought comfort and growth. For example: 'This loss hurts deeply, but God is near the brokenhearted and will carry me through (Psalm 34:18).

---

7. Talk with your partner: How has resting in Christ's love already helped shift your thinking in tough moments? How can you encourage each other to renew your minds with God's truth when negativity arises, so grace produces joy in your marriage?

EXERCISE 2

This exercise will help you and your fiancé take responsibility for your own attitudes. It will take about ten to fifteen minutes.

Blame shifts responsibility and blocks grace in marriage. Under the New Covenant, we take ownership of our attitudes and responses, not to earn God's favor (already ours in Christ), but to reflect His forgiveness and keep unity as heirs together of the grace of life (1 Peter 3:7).

Below are several scenarios where blame typically enters the picture. For each scenario, decide on your own who is to blame.

First Scene

It's Valentine's Day. Mary has prepared a special meal for Dan – all his favorite foods. She also made him a special Valentine. Dan, however, didn't get Mary anything. After dinner, Dan thanks Mary for the food and slumps into a chair in front of the television. Mary, feeling hurt, leaves the dirty dishes in the sink and goes into the bedroom to cry. Dan realizes what just happened, follows her into the bedroom, and the two accuse each other of being insensitive. Who is at fault?

Dan is to blame — Mary is to blame

Second Scene

Aaron and Kim are having dinner with another couple. During the casual conversation, Kim jokingly makes fun of Aaron's shirt. He laughs at first, but soon he becomes withdrawn, and the conversation becomes noticeably strained. When they get home, both of them accuse the other of ruining the evening. Who is at fault?

Aaron is to blame — Kim is to blame

Third Scene

On a whim, Carl buys a new 85" television on sale. He and Michelle had talked about getting one, but they decided to wait another year. Carl, however, felt the bargain was too good to pass up and also thought it would be a nice surprise for Michelle. It wasn't. All Michelle could think about was how they were saving money for plane tickets to see her family at Christmas. Carl and Michelle blamed each other for being too controlling with their money. Who is at fault.

Carl is to blame Michelle is to blame

After reading each scenario again, discuss together: How could resting in Christ's unconditional love and forgiveness help each person respond with grace instead of blame? What small step of humility or simple prayer could turn the situation toward solution and greater closeness?

EXERCISE 3

ATTITUDE EVALUATION

Have you checked your attitude lately? How would you rate your attitude:

- o My attitude often reflects Christ's joy and peace.
- o My attitude sometimes drifts to negativity, and I need to rest more in grace.
- o My attitude needs renewal through God's Word and the Holy Spirit.
- o My attitude is mostly negative, and I'm ready to invite God's transforming grace.

Take a few minutes to consider the following: Take time to pray and reflect

1. Am I resting in who I am in Christ (fully loved, complete—Colossians 2:10)?

____

2. Have I accepted God's grace for my life or become fatalistic?

____

3. Have negative words or past hurts hindered my outlook, and how can God's truth set me free?

____

____

____

____

4. Do I tend toward negativity, and how can the Holy Spirit produce joy instead (Galatians 5:22)?

____

____

5. Am I open to letting grace renew any wrong attitudes?

____

6. What situations or circumstances in your relationship so far have thrown you for a loop? Write down the particular challenges that you did not anticipate?

____

____

____

____

____

____

7. What situations in your relationship so far have surprised you? How did you respond? List positive ways you coped (e.g., prayed, remembered God's faithfulness) and ways that didn't help (e.g., complained, withdrew)

Positive ways I coped	**Negative ways I coped**
____________________	____________________
____________________	____________________
____________________	____________________
____________________	____________________
____________________	____________________
____________________	____________________
____________________	____________________
____________________	____________________
____________________	____________________
____________________	____________________

Share with your partner: How has resting in Christ's finished work already helped you adjust to surprises in your relationship? How can you encourage each other to renew your minds with God's truth when challenges arise?

Conclude by discussing: If we do not invite God's grace to renew our attitudes, how might that affect our marriage? How can depending on Him daily make "happily ever after" a living, grace-filled reality?

He Speaks Male, She Speaks Female

Happiness has no reason. It is not found in the facts of our lives, but in the color of the light by which we look at the facts. True joy isn't circumstantial: it is the fruit of resting in Christ's unchanging love!

Communication

Men and women do communicate differently, and that can create challenges. But under the New Covenant, the real power for understanding comes from resting in Christ's unconditional love for us. Because we are fully accepted in Him (Ephesians 1:6), we can offer that same acceptance and grace to our spouse—listening and speaking from security, not fear or performance.

Breakdown in communication is one of the biggest problems couples face in marriage. The health of the marriage depends on whether partners can say what they mean clearly and understand what they hear accurately. The best time to build these skills is now, while things are going well.

These misfires often happen when we operate from self-protection instead of Christ's love. Grace removes fear (1 John 4:18), making honest exchange safe and freeing.

HOW NOT TO COMMUNICATE

Many couples in troubled marriages believe that the fact they don't talk anymore is the cause of their problems. In fact, silence is not a lack of communication but a powerful form of it, sending negative messages in abundance.

Good communication is built first on who you are–and only later on what you do. You can read articles and books that will teach you communication skills, but if you do not first focus on the personal qualities you possess as a partner, your efforts will be in vain.

Silence is not the cause of poor communication—the fear of pain is. Human nature seeks pleasure and avoids pain. People avoid pain first and then seek pleasure. This is crucial to understanding communication breakdown, because it occurs when we urgently want to avoid the emotional pain of feeling inadequate, vulnerable, fearful, or blamed.

Under these potentially painful circumstances, communication goes awry. When we feel inadequate, we communicate, "If you really knew what I was like, you might not like me." When fearful: "If I expressed my anger, it would destroy you" or "If I told you how I felt, you would get angry."

Defensive communicative styles often come from feeling unsafe or unworthy. In Christ, we are already secure and loved—no need to protect ourselves through appeasing, blaming, calculating, or diverting. Grace makes it safe to be honest and vulnerable, because Christ's acceptance covers us (Romans 8:1—no condemnation).

These defensive styles naturally fade as we rest in Christ's acceptance. There is no need to protect or perform when we know we are already loved.

Following below are the four most common styles of miscommunication that result when we feel threatened:

1. **Appeaser**

The appeaser is a yes-person, ingratiating, eager to please, and apologetic, with a "sorry to be alive" attitude. They say things like "Whatever you want" or "Don't worry about me, it's okay." They want to keep the peace at all costs, but the price they pay is a feeling of worthlessness. Appeasers often bottle up anger and can struggle with depression.

If you recognize yourself here, rest in your worth in Christ. You don't have to earn love—it is freely given.

2. **Blamer**

The blamer is a nitpicker and faultfinder who criticizes relentlessly and speaks in generalizations: "You never do anything right" or "You are just like your mother/father." Deep down, blamers feel unworthy and unlovable, angry at the anticipation that they won't get what they want. The best defense, they believe, is attack.

If this is you, grace empowers you to own your part without attacking (Philippians 2:3–4). You can speak on your own behalf without indicting others.

3. **Calculator**

The calculator is super-reasonable, calm, and collected, never admits mistakes, and expects others to conform and perform. They say things like "Upset? I'm not upset. What makes you think I'm upset?" Afraid of emotion, they prefer facts and statistics: "I don't show my emotions, and I'm not interested in anyone else's."

Christ felt deeply—He wept (John 11:35). Grace invites us to share emotions honestly.

4. **Diverter**

The diverter resorts to irrelevancies when cornered, avoiding direct eye contact and direct answers. They master changing the subject: "What problem? Let's do lunch." Confronting the problem might lead to a fight, which feels dangerous, so they ignore it.

Grace gives courage to face issues, knowing God works all things for good (Romans 8:28))

FOUNDATION INGREDIENTS

Let us establish what the ingredients are for a solid communication foundation - those ingredients that will set the scene and create a safe environment for effective communication:

1. Acceptance

Your partner came into the marriage with a whole bunch of qualities—some known, many still to be discovered—yet you have chosen to embrace them warts and all. That is what unconditional acceptance and personal warmth are made of.

Rather than requiring change, you simply and unconditionally accept the thoughts, feelings, and actions of the person you love. Acceptance and warmth invite your partner to be who they are—relaxed, free, and at peace. It boosts confidence and prevents the misery of contorting personality to win approval.

The biggest gift you can give your partner is permission to be who they really are. Unconditional acceptance invites God's grace into the soul of your marriage. When your partner feels secure that they will never be condemned for who they are, grace seeps into the fabric of your relationship. After all, God did not expect us to clean up our act first before He accepted us as children. He accepted us unconditionally—warts and all—through Christ (Romans 5:8).

2. Authenticity

Partners have built-in radars for detecting falseness. Your partner will not trust you if they feel you are not genuine. Authenticity is expressed not so much by what you say but by how you say it—through tone of voice, facial expression, and posture.

Your marriage does not need your interpretation of the perfect spouse; it needs the real you. Authenticity is something you are, not something you do. It comes from the heart. Authenticity flows from being secure in who we are in Christ—no need to pretend.

3. Empathy

The best way to avoid stepping on your partner's toes is to walk a mile in their shoes. Seeing the world from your partner's perspective is empathy.

We should never assume our partner knows what we are experiencing. Everyone interprets life from their own unique insights. Life looks different for them than it does for us. Only after entering their world with both head and heart can we accurately understand their perspective.

Empathy brings together both heart and head to fully understand our partner. It says, "If I were you, I would feel the same; I understand why you feel the way you feel." It reflects Christ, who became like us to understand us fully (Hebrews 4:15). Grace empowers us to enter our spouse's world without fixing or judging.

These three qualities—acceptance, authenticity, and empathy—are critical, but they work best when combined with the practical skills of listening, talking, and touching.

HOW CAN I SAY: "I LOVE YOU" IF I NEVER <u>LISTEN</u> TO WHO YOU ARE?

A wise man once said the Lord gave us two ears and one mouth, and that ratio should tell us something! We often think good communication is about expressing ourselves more effectively. In reality, ninety-eight percent of good communication is listening.

Good listening is a form of dying to self (Philippians 2:3–4)—putting aside our own agenda to reflect Christ's attentive love. As we rest in the reality that He listens to us, we become better able to listen to our spouse.

Statistics show that only 7 percent of a message comes across in words, 50 percent through body language and facial expressions, and 43 percent through tone of voice. A good listener is often the one who first opens the door to healthy communication.

Hearing is passive. Listening is actively interacting with the message by reflecting it back to the sender. It is becoming a mirror for someone, reflecting back an image of who that person is in your eyes. This takes self-control. James 1:19 says, "Be quick to listen, slow to speak."

How to Practice Effective Listening:

1. <u>Focus your attention on the speaker–for his/her benefit</u>

Let them know you are interested. Switch off distractions, look them in the eye, lean slightly toward them, and use encouraging nods or simple affirming words such as "Yes," "uh-huh," or "I see." Sit with an open posture—unfold your arms and legs. This sends the message that you are welcoming them into your space.

2. <u>Focus your attention on the speaker – for your benefit</u>

Remember that words convey only 7 percent of the message. Pay attention to body language—the folded arms, smile, frown, laughter, or tears.

3. <u>Keep your mind on the subject at hand</u>

Resist the temptation to compose your response while the other person is still speaking.

4. <u>Ask questions to get more information</u>

There is no greater lie than a truth misunderstood. Ask clarifying questions such as "Do you mean...?" or "Are you saying...?" Ask for permission first: "May I ask you a question?" Use open questions beginning with "what," "how," "when," or "where." Avoid "why" questions, which can sound accusatory

5. <u>Practice reflective listening (LUV talk)</u>

The point of reflective listening is to let your partner know you have heard them and understand their message. You check for accuracy: "I heard you say that... Am I right?"

Gary Smalley calls this LUV Talk. Like a fast-food employee repeating your order, you reflect back what you heard—both the content and the feelings—without adding advice or criticism. This clarifies the conversation, prevents misunderstanding, and allows couples to delve into deeper meanings. The listener does not have to agree or change behavior on the spot. Once the speaker feels understood and validated, roles can reverse.

Simple rules for LUV Talk:

- Listen
- Understand
- Validate
- Repeat

HOW CAN I KNOW WHO YOU ARE IF YOU ARE NOT TALKING?

"Do not let any unwholesome talk come out of your mouths but only what is helpful for building others up according to their needs." Ephesians 4:29.

Some of us, quiet by nature, will always find it easier to listen than to speak. To be a good communicator one doesn't have to become a professional athlete of the tongue. On the other hand, a quiet nature isn't an escape mechanism for non-communication. To minimize misunderstanding, you and your spouse need to learn to verbalize as clearly as possible, what is going on inside of you?

Five levels of communication can be distinguished:

Level 1: Cliché, greeting – polite small-talk that often may not need a response.

Level 2: Reporting facts. "The washing machine is broken." Your report may or may not lead to longer conversation.

Level 3: Rational discussion, sharing of your interpretation of events. The arena now widens from facts to opinions, which are an important part of who you are. Because this opens the door to arguments and disagreements, we are a little more selective in our audience.

Most of our day-to-day conversation remains on the first three levels and occurs without much effort, thought or risk.

Level 4: This involves the sharing of feelings and emotions. In a recent survey of 3000 women asked what they would most like to change about men. The number one response was that men should be more able to express their feelings.

Level 5: Intimate, emotional communication. This includes the other levels but goes beyond them to sharing the roots of the feelings, the dreams of the future and memories of the past, the reasons for feelings such as success and shame, fear and joy.

Keep in mind that Jesus freely expressed His emotions – joy (Luke 10:21), sorrow and tears (Luke 19:41).

Skills for Good Communication

1. Using "I" instead of "You" messages

"Death and life are in the power of the tongue." (Proverbs 18:21)

When hurt or upset, our natural tendency is to attack with "You-statements": "You drive me up the wall! You never ask my opinion!" This guarantees a defensive response. An "I-message" gives information to be understood rather than accusations to be defended: "I feel hurt and neglected when you don't ask my opinion." "I" messages focus on your feelings and needs, not on your spouse's behavior or motives.

Communication is not what you say, but what your partner understands by what you say. When you send "You-messages," all your partner hears is blame and criticism. "I-messages" are much more effective and tell your partner exactly how you feel and what you want. This message focuses on your feelings and needs and not on the other's behavior and motives.

2. Accept The Differences Between Men And Women

Women often use conversation to form and strengthen connections. Men tend to use words to navigate hierarchy, communicate knowledge, and impart information. Women generally use far more words per day than men. Men tend to be linear and solution-focused; women often connect through sharing feelings.

Grace honors both styles—men often lean toward solutions, women toward connection. Neither is wrong; both reflect how God made us. The Holy Spirit helps us value and understand each other's way of communicating. Labeling a conversation "feeling-talk" or "problem-talk" can reduce frustration and honor both gifts.

3. Apologize When Necessary

A sincere apology is a powerful tool for resolving issues and strengthening relationships. It should not be used to short-circuit arguments and avoid real issues.

True apology flows from grace—we can own mistakes because Christ's blood already covers us (1 John 1:9). We can extend forgiveness freely just as we have been forgiven (Ephesians 4:32).

HOW CAN I KNOW YOU LOVE ME IF YOU DON'T TOUCH ME?

"Words! Words! I'm so sick of words! ... If you're in love, show me!" —Eliza Doolittle in My Fair Lady

Physical touch is a powerful means of communicating love and nourishing the spirit. Infants cannot thrive without it, and that need does not disappear when we grow up. Human skin is dotted with millions of touch receptors that send messages to the brain, which then secrete chemicals appropriate to the situation.

Touch communicates: "You are important," "I love you," "I'm sorry." For many couples about to marry, affectionate touch is constant. They often assume it will always be that way. Yet once children arrive, pure affectionate touching can be left behind. Remember: touching may be the best way of speaking to your partner when words fail.

FOOD FOR THOUGHT

If there is something you need to say to your loved one, say it lovingly, as if holding their heart in your hands.

EXERCISE ONE - (Women's Exercise)

HOW WELL DO YOU COMMUNICATE?

This self-test is designed to help you assess how well you communicate with your partner. Answer the questions as honestly as you can – the more honest you are, the more meaningful this exercise will be..

1. The anniversary of your first date is coming up. You have always remembered it and it is important to you, but your partner often forgets. So you:

   A. Wait to see if he'll remember.

   B. Drop hints

   C. Remind him

2. If you have a problem with your partner, with whom will you first discuss it?

   A. No one

   B. A friend or close relative.

   C. Him

3. He really hurt your feelings. Do you:

   A. Tell him so?

   B. Give him the cold shoulder for a while?

   C. Lash out and hurt him back.

4. If something terribly embarrassing happened to you, would you tell your partner about it.

   A. No

   B. Maybe

   C. Probably

5. Football bores you to death, but your partner could discuss it for hours. When the subject comes up, do you:

   A. Explain how bored you are and ask him to talk about something else.

   B. Change the subject as soon as possible?

   C. Work on showing some interest?

6. You had an unsuccessful job interview at lunchtime, and you're very upset. When you see your partner later, he looks downcast. Do you:

   A. Wait until he's in a better mood to tell him about it.

   B. Tell him but try to hide your emotions.

   C. Begin pouring out your story the moment you see him.

7. For the second time this month your partner has broken a promise to take you to a movie. Do you:

   A. Break a promise you've made to see how he likes it?

   B. Sulk and tell him how inconsiderate he is?

   C. Adjust to the letdown and tell him you are annoyed?

Scoring: For questions 1,2,4,5,7 give yourself one point for each "A: answer. Two Points for each "B" answer and three points for each "C" answer. On Questions 3 and 6, give yourself three points for each "A" answer, two points for each "B You're" answer and one point for each "C" answer.

7 – 11 points: Areas where grace can bring more openness and patience.

12-17 points: Growing, but grace can soften sensitive spots.

18-21 points: Grace is flowing well—keep resting in Christ to fine-tune.

EXERCISE ONE - (Men's Exercise)

HOW WELL DO YOU COMMUNICATE?

This self-test is designed to help you assess how well you communicate with your partner. Answer the questions as honestly as you can – the more honest you are, the more meaningful this exercise will be.

1. When your wife/partner is a bad mood, you are likely to:

   A. Ask whether she's getting her period

   B. Leave her alone until she's feeling better?

   C. Ask her what's wrong?

2. She says you don't tell her often enough that you love her. You reply"

   A. "I tell you I love you all the time"

   B. "You know I love you. Why do I have to say it?"

   C. "I love you very much. Sometimes I just forget to say it."

3. You are watching television and she says she'd like to talk to you. You say:

   A. "How about ten o'clock"

   B. "anytime you want"

   C. "Sorry, I'm in the middle of something right now."

4. How often do you do you win arguments with your partner?

   A. Almost always

   B. Almost never

   C. I try not to think in terms of winning or losing.

5. Your wife wants to talk about some difficulties she's having at work. Would you most likely:

   A. Point out that you have problems of your own?

   B. Offer helpful advice?

   C. Listen and try to be supportive.

6. For the second time this week you find that she didn't run an errand as she had promised. Annoyed, you:

   A. Tell her how much it irritates you and do it yourself.

   B. Pout a bit and ask her to do it tomorrow.

   C. "Forget to do something for her next time she asks.

7. You're in a romantic mood, but when you reach for her she just yawns. You:

   A. Feel rejected and say: "wow, it's cold in here."

   B. Ask her why she isn't responding.

   C. Let her know your desires but adjust if she doesn't feel the same.

Scoring: For questions 1,2,4,5,7 give yourself one point for each "A: answer. Two Points for each "B" answer and three points for each "C" answer. On Questions 3 and 6, give yourself three points for each "A" answer, two points for each "B" answer and one point for each "C" answer.

7 – 11 points: Areas where grace can bring more openness and patience.

12-17 points: Growing, but grace can soften sensitive spots.

18-21 points: Grace is flowing well—keep resting in Christ to fine-tune.

EXERCISE TWO

THE DAILY TEMPERATURE READING

This exercise will help you and your partner maintain an easy flow of communication about major and minor issues going on in your lives. At first this might seem a little artificial but in time you'll find that it is invaluable for staying close.

This simple practice keeps grace flowing in your marriage. Appreciation reflects gratitude to God and to each other. Sharing keeps you connected as heirs together of the grace of life (1 Peter 3:7). Even complaints can be expressed gently because of Christ's kindness toward us.

Do it daily, perhaps during a meal. Here are the basics. Sit close, holding each other's hands, then follow these five steps:

- **Appreciation**: Take turns expressing appreciation for something your partner or spouse has done. Thank each other.
- **New information**: In the absence of information, assumptions (often false ones) rush in. Tell your spouse or partner something new. Let your partner in on your life. Then listen to the news your partner shares.
- **Puzzles**: Take turns asking each other something you don't understand but your partner can explain: "Why were you so down last night?" Or voice concern about yourself: "I don't know why I got so angry when I was balancing the checkbook yesterday."
- **Complaint with request**: Without being judgmental, cite a specific behavior you are asking for instead. "When you clean the top of the stove, please dry it properly, otherwise it leaves streaks."
- **Hopes**: Share hopes, from the mundane to the grandiose.

These simple steps work for many couples who want to keep the channels of communication open.

EXERCISE THREE (Women's exercise)

I CAN HEAR CLEARLY NOW

Your partner will often hide important feelings behind his words. Reflecting his feelings is one of the most helpful and difficult listening techniques to implement. It shows empathy, mirroring how Christ hears and understands our hearts (Hebrews 4:15). Grace helps us listen without fixing or judging.

Following are some statements that a husband might make. Read each separately, listening for feelings. Make note of the feeling you hear and write your response, which reflects that feeling for each of the statements.

1. "I can't believe you agreed to go on this outing tonight without asking me first."

___

2. "Can't I relax a minute before we go out again?"

___

3. "Why can't you get ready the same time I do? It seems like I'm always waiting for you."

___

4. "Everyone at work seems to be getting ahead except me."

___

5. "What's the use? I can't seem to get through to her, so why try?"

___

6. "I feel like I'm failing at everything lately — at work, as a husband, even as a man."

___

Now compare your list of reflective statements to those listed below to see how accurately you recognized feelings. Give yourself 2 points on those items where your choice closely matches, 1 point on items where your choice only partially matches and 0 points if you missed it altogether.

Possible responses to the exercise in Active Listening:

1. "Sounds like you are feeling betrayed."
2. "Sounds like you need some time to calm down and recover."
3. "You sound frustrated. I appreciate your patience."
4. "You must feel like you're getting passed over."
5. "Sounds like you're giving up hope."

How you rate on recognizing feelings:

8 - 10 Grace is helping you hear hearts well.

5 – 7 Growing in grace—keep practicing.

0 – 4 Invite the Holy Spirit to sharpen this gift.

EXERCISE THREE (Men's exercise)

I CAN HEAR CLEARLY NOW

Your partner will often hide important feelings behind her words. Reflecting her feelings is one of the most helpful and difficult, listening techniques to implement.

Reflecting feelings shows empathy, mirroring how Christ hears and understands our hearts (Hebrews 4:15). Grace helps us listen without fixing or judging.

Following are some statements that a wife might make. Read each separately, listening for feelings. Make note of the feeling you hear and write your response, which reflects that feeling for each of the statements.

1. "I can't believe you agreed to go to this sporting event without asking me first."

___

2. "Do we have to watch football again?"

___

3. "Why do you always wait until the last minute to get ready?"

___

4. "Everyone at work seems to be getting ahead except me."

___

5. "What's the use? I keep asking him to fix it and he keeps ignoring me, so why try?"

___

6. "Sometimes I feel like I'm not enough — no matter how hard I try, I just can't seem to get it all right."

___

Now compare your list of reflective statements to those listed below to see how accurately you recognized feelings. Give yourself 2 points on those items where your choice closely matches, 1 point on items where your choice only partially matches and 0 points if you missed it altogether.

Possible responses to the exercise in Active Listening:

1. "Sounds like you are feeling betrayed."
2. "Sounds like you need some time to calm down and recover."
3. "You sound frustrated. I appreciate your patience."
4. "You must feel like you're getting passed over."
5. "Sounds like you're giving up hope."

How you rate on recognizing feelings:

8 - 10 Grace is helping you hear hearts well.

5 – 7 Growing in grace—keep practicing.

0 – 4 Invite the Holy Spirit to sharpen this gift.

EXERCISE FOUR

This isn't a performance review—it's a grace mirror. Rate honestly first yourself and then your partner, then celebrate where grace is flowing and invite God to grow you both.

Your Communication Skills	Never			Sometimes				Often		
Verbally express love	1	2	3	4	5	6	7	8	9	10
Listen sincerely and attentively	1	2	3	4	5	6	7	8	9	10
Talk too much	1	2	3	4	5	6	7	8	9	10
Discuss situations logically	1	2	3	4	5	6	7	8	9	10
Share intimately	1	2	3	4	5	6	7	8	9	10
Share goals and dreams	1	2	3	4	5	6	7	8	9	10
Give nonsexual touches in communication	1	2	3	4	5	6	7	8	9	10
Provide encouragement	1	2	3	4	5	6	7	8	9	10
Address conflict appropriately	1	2	3	4	5	6	7	8	9	10
Avoid addressing conflict	1	2	3	4	5	6	7	8	9	10
Honestly express emotions	1	2	3	4	5	6	7	8	9	10

Rate your Partner's Communication Skills	Never			Sometimes				Often		
Verbally express love	1	2	3	4	5	6	7	8	9	10
Listen sincerely and attentively	1	2	3	4	5	6	7	8	9	10
Talk too much	1	2	3	4	5	6	7	8	9	10
Discuss situations logically	1	2	3	4	5	6	7	8	9	10
Share intimately	1	2	3	4	5	6	7	8	9	10
Share goals and dreams	1	2	3	4	5	6	7	8	9	10
Give nonsexual touches in communication	1	2	3	4	5	6	7	8	9	10
Provide encouragement	1	2	3	4	5	6	7	8	9	10
Address conflict appropriately	1	2	3	4	5	6	7	8	9	10
Avoid addressing conflict	1	2	3	4	5	6	7	8	9	10
Honestly express emotions	1	2	3	4	5	6	7	8	9	10

Share lovingly: How does resting in Christ's acceptance change the way we view each other's strengths and growth areas? Celebrate the growth that comes from His finished work and invite the Holy Spirit to produce His fruit in your communication (Galatians 5:22–23).

Celebrate growth from His finished work; invite the Holy Spirit to produce fruit (Galatians 5:22-23).

What Color is the Sky on Your Planet

"Why can't a woman be more like a man?"

Henry Higgins in My Fair Lady

Male And Female He Created Them (Gen 1:27)

"And the Lord God said, 'It is not good that man should be alone; I will make him a helper comparable to him.'" (Genesis 2:18, NKJV)

God, in His infinite wisdom, created a very different being—a woman—to complement Adam. Viva la différence!

No other season of life makes the differences between men and women as obvious as marriage—and we are not talking only about physical differences. In recent years, scientists have confirmed what Scripture has always shown: men and women have different biological, physiological, and psychological realities.

God designed us male and female on purpose so we could complement each other and reflect His image in unity. Marriage only truly works with God's kind of love—unconditional, chosen by faith, not by feelings or performance. Resting in Christ's finished work frees us to delight in our differences instead of resenting them.

The contrast between the sexes is so striking it almost seems surprising that the attraction is so strong. Yet when a man and a woman marry, there is an inherent completeness. We often choose a partner who supplies what we lack. When we are weak, they are strong. When we are discouraged, they are hopeful. Because the two have become one, marriage brings a beautiful wholeness.

To make marriage thrive, we must recognize that God made us different and choose to appreciate those differences rather than try to eliminate them. Appreciating our differences actually increases intimacy as we delight in the unique way God has wired our spouse. Every human being has a deep need to be understood.

IN WHAT WAYS ARE WE DIFFERENT?

Men often pursue solutions and goals (reflecting God's provision and protection); women often seek connection and emotional closeness (reflecting God's nurturing care). Neither is superior—both are gifts from the Creator. Grace empowers us to value each other's style without demanding conformity, as we abide in Christ's love (John 15:4–5).

IN WHAT WAY CAN WE CELEBRATE THE DIFFERENCES?

Because we are already secure and complete in Christ, we are free to love and honor our spouse without needing to earn anything. Grace empowers us to meet each other's heart needs—not to fix or control, but simply to reflect Christ's love.

Instead of turning to the world's ideas about what men and women "need," let's look at what God says in His Word. Ephesians 5 gives us one of the clearest pictures of marriage in the New Covenant. Here it is in The Message paraphrase:

"Wives, understand and support your husbands in ways that show your support for Christ. The husband provides leadership to his wife the way Christ does to his church, not by domineering but by cherishing. So just as the church submits to Christ as he exercises such leadership, wives should likewise submit to their husbands. Husbands, go all out in your love for your wives, exactly as Christ did for the church—a love marked by giving, not getting. Christ's love makes the church whole. His words evoke her beauty. Everything he does and says is designed to bring the best out of her, dressing her in dazzling white silk, radiant with holiness. And that is how husband's ought to love their wives. They're really doing themselves a favor—since they're already "one" in marriage. No one abuses his own body, does he? No, he feeds and pampers it. That's how Christ treats us, the church, since we are part of his body. And this is why a man leaves father and mother and cherishes his wife. No longer two, they become "one flesh." This is a huge mystery, and I don't pretend to understand it all. What is clearest to me is the way Christ treats the church. And this provides a good picture of how each husband is to treat his wife, loving himself in loving her, and how each wife is to honor her husband."

This passage is not about rigid rules or performance. It is about reflecting the gospel. In Christ's finished work on the cross, both husband and wife are already fully loved, accepted, complete, and righteous (Colossians 2:10; Ephesians 1:6; 2 Corinthians 5:21). This is the firm foundation God wants you both to stand on. From this place of rest and security in Him, you are free to love, honor, and cherish each other — not to get something back, but because His love has already been poured into your hearts by the Holy Spirit (Romans 5:5).

A couple of things that I have learnt after being married for more than 30 years:

- Wives want to be cherished by their husbands, i.e. intentional, protective, committed, tender care. Not like the world defines cherished, which is to hold something dear - like a photograph of his grandmother. We want to be heard, and valued as a partner, not fixed or managed like a problem.
- Husbands want to be respected for their leadership, understood and supported. Christ has placed the husband over the wife as a covering, not to dominated but to protect and guide like Jesus does His church.

Here are the key truths God wants every husband and wife to know and live from as you prepare for marriage:

A. <u>You are already fully loved and accepted in Christ — your spouse does not complete you</u>

God wants you to know that your deepest identity, worth, and security come from Jesus, not from your husband or wife. You are not half a person waiting to be made whole. You are complete in Him (Colossians 2:10). When both of you rest in this truth, you stop looking to each other to fill needs that only Christ can fill. You enter marriage from fullness, not emptiness. This frees you to give love generously, without demands or score-keeping.

Grace says: "I don't need you to make me feel worthy — I already am in Christ. Now I can love you freely."

B. Marriage is a covenant of grace, not a contract of performance

God designed marriage as an unbreakable covenant that reflects Christ's eternal commitment to His bride, the church (Ephesians 5:25–32). Christ never leaves us, never stops loving us, and never bases His love on our performance. He loved us "while we were still sinners" (Romans 5:8). God wants husbands and wives to rest in this same grace toward each other — no "if you do this, then I'll do that."

Grace says: "I choose to love and honor you because Christ first loved me. My commitment flows from His unchanging covenant, not from what you do or don't do."

C. You are heirs together of the grace of life

God calls husbands and wives to live as "heirs together of the grace of life" (1 Peter 3:7). This means you share equally in God's grace, favor, and blessing. When you honor and understand each other, your prayers are not hindered and grace flows freely. When you demand, control, or resent, grace is blocked.

God wants you to know: Mutual respect, kindness, and grace-filled listening release blessing over your home. You are partners, not competitors — both loved, both valued, both empowered by the same Spirit.

D. Differences are God's good design - celebrate them under grace

God made you male and female on purpose (Genesis 1:27). The ways you think, feel, communicate, and recharge are not accidents — they are gifts. A husband may lean toward goals and solutions; a wife may lean toward connection and feelings. Neither is wrong; both reflect God's creativity.

Grace helps you stop trying to change each other into your own image. Instead, rest in Christ and let the Holy Spirit produce patience, kindness, and understanding (Galatians 5:22–23). Celebrate what makes your spouse different — it is part of the completeness God planned.

E. Love and honor flow from resting in Christ - not striving

God does not want you to try harder to be a "good husband" or "good wife" in your own strength. He wants you to abide in Jesus (John 15:4–5). As you rest in His finished work — His perfect love, His complete acceptance — the Holy Spirit naturally produces the fruit of love, joy, patience, kindness, and self-control in your marriage.

Grace says: "I don't have to manufacture love or fix my spouse. I rest in how much Jesus loves me, and His love flows through me to you."

F. Forgiveness and grace cover every failure

God wants you to know that Christ's blood already covers every sin (1 John 1:7–9). You are forgiven, so you can forgive quickly and freely (Ephesians 4:32). Above all, "love covers a multitude of sins" (1 Peter 4:8). Resentment, blame, or score-keeping blocks grace; quick forgiveness and mercy release it.

God's heart is that your home would be a place of grace, where failures become opportunities to point each other back to the cross. Love — the kind that flows from Christ's finished work — covers over the inevitable mistakes, weaknesses, and shortcomings we all bring into marriage. When you choose to forgive and extend mercy, you are living out the gospel in your home.

G. Your marriage is meant to reflect Christ's love to the World

God wants your marriage to be a living testimony: "Look how much Jesus loves His church!" (Ephesians 5:32). When you rest in grace, honor differences, listen with empathy, cherish and appreciate each other, forgive freely, and stay committed "no matter what," the world sees a picture of Christ's unbreakable, grace-filled love.

This is not about being perfect — it is about being authentic, resting in Christ, and letting His love shine through your imperfections.

FOOD FOR THOUGHT

You don't have to earn love, fix each other, or perform perfectly. In Christ, you are already loved, accepted, complete, and empowered by grace. From that secure place, you can freely love, honor, understand, and celebrate your spouse. Differences become gifts. Challenges become opportunities to depend on grace. Your marriage becomes a safe, joyful place where both of you grow closer to Jesus and to each other.

Rest in His finished work. Let His grace do the heavy lifting and produce mutual honor and joy. Watch how He makes "two become one" in ways far beyond what you could achieve on your own.

EXERCISE ONE

This exercise is best done after you are married, as real-life patterns emerge. It helps you see the roles, contributions, and needs that show up in your relationship—some you chose, some you inherited unconsciously.

Under grace, remember: your value and importance in this marriage don't come from what you do or how well you 'play your role.' You are already fully loved, accepted, and complete in Christ (Colossians 2:10).

From that secure place, you are free to serve, love, and honor each other—not to earn anything, but because Christ's love overflows through you. Use this exercise to celebrate how God made you different and to invite His grace to shape your partnership.

Complete the following sentences as honestly as you can:

1. Example: I am important to our marriage because God created me in His image and placed me here to reflect His love with you.

2. What I enjoy contributing to our life together is:

___

___

3. I feel central to our relationship when:

___

___

4. I feel peripheral to our relationship when:

___

___

5. The ways I have fun with you are:

___

___

6. The way I recharge or get healthy space for myself is:

7. The ways I am intimate with you are:

8. The ways I love and serve you are:

9. I feel most feminine / masculine in our relationship when:

10. I deal with stress by:

11. How we share household responsibilities feels most balanced when:

12. How we handle finances together feels most secure when:

____

____

____

____

13. How we enjoy our spare time together is best when:

____

____

____

____

14. Our social life feels most enjoyable when:

____

____

____

15. I need you to:

____

____

____

____

Compare your statements with each other and discuss how your gender influences the way you respond. These reflect God's wiring, but ultimate fulfillment is in Christ (Colossians. 2:10).

EXERCISE TWO

YOUR TOP TEN NEEDS

This exercise helps you become aware of some of the important ways you feel loved and valued in marriage. Remember: your deepest need—for love, acceptance, security, and worth—is already fully met in Christ (Colossians 2:10; Ephesians 1:6). You are complete in Him. Because of this, you can share your heart needs with your spouse from a place of security, not desperation. This isn't about demanding or fixing each other—it's about learning how to love and honor one another more freely under God's grace. Do this on your own first, then share openly and listen without judging.

Rate how important each feels to you right now. There are no right or wrong answers—God wired each of you uniquely. These are ways you feel most loved and secure, but your ultimate security and fulfilment is already in Christ. Grace helps us meet these needs for each other without pressure or score-keeping.

Need	**Not that important**				**Very important**		
Admiration	1	2	3	4	5	6	7
Affection	1	2	3	4	5	6	7
Commitment	1	2	3	4	5	6	7
Conversation	1	2	3	4	5	6	7
Companionship	1	2	3	4	5	6	7
Financial Support	1	2	3	4	5	6	7
Honesty	1	2	3	4	5	6	7
Intimacy	1	2	3	4	5	6	7
Personal Space	1	2	3	4	5	6	7
Respect	1	2	3	4	5	6	7
Security	1	2	3	4	5	6	7
Shared activity	1	2	3	4	5	6	7
Sex	1	2	3	4	5	6	7

Now rank your top needs in order of importance for you personally. Then share your lists with each other. Discuss together:

- Which needs overlap? Celebrate those shared values!
- Where do you see differences? How might those reflect God's good design in each of you?
- What does each top need really look like in everyday life for you? (Be specific: 'affection' might mean a hug for one, words of love for the other.)
- How can resting in Christ's finished work—knowing you are already fully loved—help you give and receive these needs without fear or demands?

End by praying together: 'Lord Jesus, thank You that our deepest needs are met in You. Help us rest in Your love so we can love and honor each other freely. Show us how to meet each other's heart needs with grace and joy. Amen

Round #1: Staying in the Ring

Marriage was made in heaven, but then... so was thunder and lightning!

How To Fight A Good Fight

Many Christian couples believe that if Jesus is first in their marriage, they will live in constant peace and harmony—no arguments, no tension. That is a myth. Even with Christ at the center, disagreements happen. Why? Because God made husbands and wives wonderfully different (Genesis 1:27; see Session 5). Those different ways of thinking, feeling, and communicating do not disappear when you say "I do." They are part of God's good design.

Harmony is a beautiful, realistic goal. Paul writes in Philippians 2:2 to be "like-minded, having the same love, being one in spirit and of one mind." This applies especially to two people who have become "one flesh." But harmony under the New Covenant does not mean never disagreeing. It means learning to disagree in ways that reflect Christ's love.

The absence of conflict is not proof of a strong marriage. In fact, avoiding conflict often weakens it. When couples never address differences, hurts build up silently until they explode or create distance. The number one predictor of divorce is not fighting—it is habitual avoidance of conflict.

Strife enters when we operate from conditional love—demanding our way or punishing faults. But God's kind of love, received by grace through the Cross, prefers the other (Philippians 2:3–4), diffuses tension, and turns differences into opportunities for oneness.

God wants something better for you. Successful couples—those whose marriages grow stronger over time—learn to handle disagreements in ways that actually deepen intimacy and trust. Conflict is not a crisis to fear; it is an opportunity to grow closer to Christ and to each other. When you rest in His finished work, knowing you are already fully loved and accepted (Ephesians 1:6), you do not have to win arguments or protect yourself. The Holy Spirit can produce patience, kindness, and self-control (Galatians 5:22–23), helping you listen, forgive, and resolve issues with love.

Every happy, long-term marriage has about ten ongoing differences that are never fully resolved. Successful couples do not try to eliminate them; they learn to make music together in spite of them. Your vows promise "till death do us part," not "till we become the same person." Under grace, conflict becomes a doorway to deeper oneness.

FIGHTING DIRTY

Even for born-again believers, old patterns can surface during conflict. We all have moments where our words or silence hurt instead of heal. God wants us to recognize these patterns—not to condemn ourselves (there is no condemnation in Christ—Romans 8:1), but to turn quickly to His grace. The Holy Spirit can replace destructive habits with love, patience, and kindness as we abide in Jesus.

Dr. John Gottman's research highlights four common ways couples "fight dirty" that damage intimacy. These are not signs you are a bad spouse—they are signals to run back to the cross and let grace renew your heart and words. These patterns surface when we forget our security in Christ. Resting in His unconditional acceptance (Ephesians 1:6) frees us from defensiveness or contempt—His mercy covers us, so we extend mercy (James 2:13).

1. **Criticism**

Criticism attacks who your spouse is, not what they did. It feels like a personal assault.

Healthy complaint: "I wish we could see my parents more often."

Criticism: "You never take me to see my parents—you don't care about my family."

Criticism starts with "you" and blames character. Under grace, we can learn to speak from "I feel" instead of accusing. The tongue is small but powerful—it can set a whole life on fire (James 3:5–6). Grace helps us speak life instead of death (Ephesians 4:29)

2. **Contempt**

Contempt is the most toxic of all. It mocks, ridicules, or shows disgust through name-calling, sarcasm, eye-rolling, or hostile humor. It says, "You're beneath me." It destroys respect and safety faster than almost anything else.

God wants your marriage to be a place of honor, not dishonor. Contempt grieves the Holy Spirit (Ephesians 4:30–31). When we rest in how much Christ cherishes us—warts and all—we are freed to cherish our spouse the same way, with no need to tear down in order to feel better.

3. **Defensiveness**

Defensiveness happens when we feel attacked: we counter, justify, make excuses, or play the victim ("It's not my fault," "You always...," "But you did this first...").

Defensiveness blocks responsibility and keeps conflict spinning. Grace frees us to own our part without fear. Because Christ already took our blame on the cross, we do not have to defend ourselves. We can humbly say, "I see where I hurt you. I'm sorry," and let grace heal.

4. **Stonewalling**

Stonewalling is shutting down, going silent, withdrawing, avoiding eye contact, giving one-word answers, or walking away emotionally. It often happens when someone feels overwhelmed or flooded. It sends the message: "I'm done with you." It creates icy distance.

Grace invites us to stay present, even when it is hard. Christ never withdrew from us—He pursued us to the cross. Resting in His love gives courage to say, "I need a moment to calm down, but I'm not leaving you. I love you."

These patterns are common when we rely on our own strength instead of grace. The good news: Christ's finished work covers every harsh word and every shutdown. When we confess and receive His forgiveness (1 John 1:9), grace renews our hearts. The Holy Spirit produces kindness, gentleness, and self-control (Galatians 5:22–23), helping us replace dirty fighting with grace-filled responses.

God wants your conflicts to end in reconciliation, not resentment. As you rest in His love, these old habits lose their power, and your words and silence begin to build up instead of tear down.

FIGHTING FAIR

God does not want you to avoid conflict or "win" every argument. He wants your disagreements to draw you closer to Him and to each other. Under grace, you do not have to rely on perfect technique or endless effort. As you rest in Christ's finished work—knowing you are already fully loved, accepted, and complete (Colossians 2:10)—the Holy Spirit produces the fruit needed for healthy conflict: patience, kindness, gentleness, and self-control (Galatians 5:22–23). Grace makes it safe to be honest, humble, and quick to forgive.

Here are grace-filled ways to handle disagreements that strengthen your marriage instead of tearing it down:

1. Don't retreat

It is tempting to walk away, go silent, or sweep things under the rug when conflict feels uncomfortable. But retreating builds walls and lets hurts grow. Grace invites you to stay present. Christ never withdrew from us—He pursued us to the cross. Resting in His love gives courage to stay engaged. Then you can say, "This is hard, but I love you and want to work through it together."

When tension rises, take a brief pause if needed (a few deep breaths or a short walk), but come back. Let your spouse know: "I need a moment to calm down, but I'm not leaving you—I'm committed to us." Listen attentively and try paraphrasing what you hear: "It sounds like you're feeling hurt because I didn't call when I said I would. Is that right?" This shows you value their heart and helps both feel truly heard.

2. Choose your battles with great care

Not every irritation needs a full discussion. Some things (how the toothpaste is squeezed, small habits) can be let go with love. Ask yourself: "Is this worth potential hurt? Will it matter in a week? A year?" Grace helps you release minor things, trusting God with the small stuff (Proverbs 19:11).

Focus on what truly affects your oneness—recurring hurts, unmet needs, or patterns that pull you apart. Bring those up gently, not in the heat of emotion. Choose a calm time and place (not the bedroom—keep that space for closeness). Grace reminds you: your spouse is not the enemy; the real issue is what needs grace and understanding.

3. Define the conflict clearly

Many arguments spiral because couples fight about surface things while the real issue stays hidden. Grace helps you slow down and ask: "What are we really disagreeing about?" "What hurt or need is underneath this?"

Start with "I" statements: "I feel lonely when we don't have time together," instead of "You never spend time with me." Speak truth in love (Ephesians 4:15). Let your spouse repeat what they heard until they get it right. When both feel understood, the heart of the issue becomes clear, and solutions often appear naturally.

It is not wise or profitable to bring up past conflicts or hurts that have already been resolved. When you disagree, don't fight old fights. It's like dragging an old dead cow out of a ditch—all it does is stink and make everyone feel ill. Once something has been forgiven and dealt with, leave it there. Christ's finished work has already wiped the slate clean (Colossians 2:14),and it should be the same for arguments and disagreements, once it's been dealt with, the slate should be wiped clean. Holding onto or dragging up resolved issues blocks the flow of grace and keeps you from the fresh oneness God wants for you today.

4. Brainstorm solutions together

Once feelings are heard and needs are understood, let ideas flow without judging at first—like throwing balloons "up in the air." Then evaluate together: "What feels fair and honoring to both of us?" Grace removes the need to "win." You're not opponents; you're partners, heirs together of the grace of life (1 Peter 3:7). The goal isn't getting your way; it's finding a path that values both hearts.

Sometimes no perfect solution exists. Grace helps you accept that and choose love anyway: "I don't love this outcome, but I love you more than being right." The Holy Spirit often brings creative ideas when you are both humble and open.

5. End with forgiveness and reconnection

Every healthy disagreement should have a beginning, middle, and end. When resolution comes (or even if it is partial), make up quickly. Don't let the sun go down on your anger (Ephesians 4:26). Forgiveness is a choice, not a feeling—choose it freely because Christ forgave you completely (Colossians 3:13).

Reaffirm your love: hold hands, hug, kiss, say "I love you," pray together. Grace seals the moment—turning conflict into a testimony of Christ's reconciling love.

God wants your fights to end in peace, not resentment. As you rest in His grace, old patterns lose power, and your words and actions begin to build up instead of tear down. Conflict handled under grace doesn't weaken your marriage—it strengthens it, drawing you closer to each other and to Jesus

NEGOTIATING A CEASE FIRE

When tension rises and hearts feel hurt, God wants your marriage to move toward peace, not prolonged battle. Under grace, you don't have to "win" the argument or force a perfect solution. Because Christ has already reconciled you to God through His finished work (2 Corinthians 5:18–19), the same reconciling grace can flow between you. Resting in His love frees you to listen, forgive, and restore closeness without fear or striving.

Here's how grace helps you negotiate a cease fire and return to peace:

1. Pause and Pray together

When emotions run high, take a moment to stop and pray (out loud or silently). Ask the Holy Spirit for tender hearts and wisdom. "Lord, help us see each other through Your eyes of love. Give us grace to listen and forgive." Prayer invites God into the moment and softens hearts before words are spoken. Grace reminds you: you're on the same side—partners, not enemies.

2. Share feelings and needs honestly, from a place of grace

Each of you can take a turn to express what's really going on. Use "I" statements to own your feelings:

"I feel hurt and lonely when we don't have time together."

"I feel frustrated because I wanted us to decide this together."

Avoid blame ("You always..." "You never..."). Grace helps you speak truth in love (Ephesians 4:15) without attacking character. The goal isn't to prove who is right; it's to let your spouse hear your heart.

3. Listen and reflect back with grace

After one partner shares, the other listens without interrupting. Then reflect what you heard:

"It sounds like you're feeling hurt because I didn't include you in the decision. Is that right?"

"I hear that you feel overwhelmed and need some space right now. Did I understand that correctly?"

This simple step shows: "I value you. I want to understand." Grace empowers active listening—Christ listens to us perfectly (Hebrews 4:15), and we reflect His care. When both feel truly heard, defensiveness drops and understanding grows.

4. Brainstorming solutions under Grace

Once feelings are understood, look for solutions that honor both hearts. Let ideas flow freely—no judging at first. Throw them out like balloons: "What if we tried...?" Then talk through which one feels fair and loving to both. Solutions flow when hearts are heard; grace produces creativity in unity.

If no perfect answer appears, grace helps you choose love over being right: "I don't love this outcome, but I love you more than winning." Sometimes the best solution is simply to forgive, hug, and move forward together. The Holy Spirit often brings creative ideas when both are humble and open.

5. End with forgiveness and reconnection

Every healthy disagreement needs a clear ending. When you reach understanding (even if partial), forgive quickly. Forgiveness is a choice, not a feeling—choose it freely because Christ forgave you completely (Colossians 3:13; Ephesians 4:32). Don't let the sun go down on your anger (Ephesians 4:26).

Then reaffirm your love: sit close, hold hands, hug, kiss, say "I love you," pray together. Grace seals the moment—turning hurt into closeness. A simple "I'm sorry. I love you. Let's start fresh" opens the door back to joy.

God wants your conflicts to end in peace and renewed oneness. As you rest in His grace, old patterns lose power. The Holy Spirit produces gentleness and peace, so your words and actions build up instead of tear down. Conflict handled under grace doesn't weaken your marriage—it strengthens it, showing the world a picture of Christ's reconciling love

PEACE AT LAST

A healthy disagreement should have a clear ending. When understanding comes (even if it's partial), grace helps you close the conflict with forgiveness and reconnection. God doesn't want hurt or resentment to linger. He wants your marriage to be a place of peace and joy.

Don't let the sun go down on your anger (Ephesians 4:26). Forgiveness is a choice, not a feeling. Choose to forgive quickly and freely because Christ has already forgiven you completely (Colossians 3:13; Ephesians 4:32). You don't have to wait until you "feel" forgiving, grace empowers you to release the offense, knowing Jesus took every wrong on the cross. Let go of the need to be right or get even. Rest in His finished work, and peace will follow.

When the tension lifts, reaffirm your love. Sit close, hold hands, hug, kiss, or simply look into each other's eyes and say, "I love you. I'm sorry for my part. Let's start fresh." Physical closeness—touching, embracing—reminds you both that you are safe and cherished. These small acts of reconnection reflect how Christ draws near to us in love, even after our failures.

Pray together: "Lord Jesus, thank You for Your grace that covers us. Help us forgive as You forgave us. Restore our joy and oneness. Amen." Prayer invites the Holy Spirit to seal the moment with His peace that surpasses understanding (Philippians 4:7).

Grace turns conflict into closeness. When you end disagreements this way with no lingering bitterness, quick forgiveness, tender touch, and prayer, your marriage becomes a testimony of Christ's reconciling love. The world sees: "This couple fights, but they don't stay mad. They forgive, they reconnect, they love deeply, because they rest in Jesus."

You won't always resolve every issue perfectly. That's okay. Grace covers what's unfinished. What matters is that you end with love reaffirmed, hearts soft, and Christ at the center. As you rest in His finished work, the Holy Spirit produces peace, gentleness, and joy (Galatians 5:22–23), so your home becomes a place where conflicts end in grace, not grudges.

FOOD FOR THOUGHT

"In a covenant marriage, we don't fight to win—we fight for oneness. Grace doesn't keep score; it keeps loving." Duane Sheriff

"As heirs together of the grace of life, we forgive quickly so nothing hinders our prayers or our love." Greg Mohr on 1 Peter 3:7

EXERCISE ONE

IDENTIFYING YOUR HOT TOPICS

This exercise helps you and your partner become aware of the issues that tend to cause tension in your relationship. Knowing these "hot topics" ahead of time is a gift of grace — it gives you an opportunity to invite God's peace and wisdom before things heat up.

Rate each issue on your own first (1 = not a problem at all, 7 = very much a problem). Add any other topics that come to mind. There are no right or wrong answers — God already knows your heart, and He loves you completely in Christ (Ephesians 1:6). This is simply a way to bring things into the light so grace can work in them.

Issue	**Not a problem at all**				**Very much a problem**		
Careers	1	2	3	4	5	6	7
Children	1	2	3	4	5	6	7
Chores	1	2	3	4	5	6	7
Communication	1	2	3	4	5	6	7
Friends	1	2	3	4	5	6	7
Illness	1	2	3	4	5	6	7
In-laws	1	2	3	4	5	6	7
Jealousy	1	2	3	4	5	6	7
Money	1	2	3	4	5	6	7
Priorities	1	2	3	4	5	6	7
Recreation	1	2	3	4	5	6	7
Religion	1	2	3	4	5	6	7
Sex	1	2	3	4	5	6	7
Sleep habits	1	2	3	4	5	6	7
	1	2	3	4	5	6	7
	1	2	3	4	5	6	7
	1	2	3	4	5	6	7

After you both finish rating on your own, share your lists openly and listen without judging or defending.

Discuss together:

- Which topics are "hot" for both of you? Celebrate the overlap—those shared values can become strengths in your marriage.
- Which ones are hotter for one of you than the other? How might these reflect the beautiful differences God built into you (Genesis 1:27)?
- Are any of these likely to become more intense after marriage (money, in-laws, children, etc.)?
- How can resting in Christ's finished work—knowing you are already fully loved and secure in Him (Colossians 2:10)—help you approach these topics with grace instead of fear or frustration?
- What small step of grace could you take together now (prayer, a kind conversation, setting a boundary) to invite God's peace before tension builds?

End by praying together (keep it simple):

"Lord Jesus, thank You that Your grace is bigger than any conflict we'll face. Help us rest in Your love so we can face these hot topics with patience, kindness, and forgiveness. Show us how to honor each other as heirs together of the grace of life (1 Peter 3:7). Amen."

EXERCISE TWO

SHARING WITHHOLDS

This simple daily practice helps you keep a clean emotional slate and prevents small hurts from building into bigger conflicts. It gives you a safe way to share thoughts and feelings you might otherwise hold back — before they turn into resentment or assumptions.

Under grace, you don't have to hide hurt or pretend everything is fine. Because Christ has already forgiven you completely (Colossians 3:13), you are free to be honest without fear of rejection. And because you are both fully loved and accepted in Him (Ephesians 1:6), you can receive each other's words with tenderness, not defensiveness. This short habit invites God's grace to keep your hearts soft and your connection strong.

How to do it

Do this daily, if possible (it only takes 2–3 minutes), ideally over a meal or before bed. Sit close, hold hands if it feels natural. Take turns following these steps:

1. **Appreciation**: Each share **two** things your partner did in the last 24–48 hours that you sincerely appreciated but didn't mention at the time.
    - Example: "I appreciated how you smiled at me when I walked in last night — it made me feel seen."
2. **One withhold**: Share **one** thing your partner did (or didn't do) in the last 24–48 hours that irritated, hurt, or bothered you, but you didn't say anything about it at the time. Keep it specific, gentle, and recent. Example:
    - "Yesterday when you kept scrolling on your phone while I was talking about my day, I felt a little dismissed."

Important grace rule:

The person listening responds only with "Thank you." No defending, explaining, or fixing—just "Thank you."

This keeps the moment safe. The one sharing feels heard. The one listening practices humility, trusting Christ's grace to cover any imperfection.

Close with a simple prayer or reflection: "Thank You, Lord, that Your love covers every small hurt. Help us keep our hearts open and quick to forgive as we rest in Your finished work. Amen."

EXERCISE THREE

FIGHTING A FAIR FIGHT

This exercise will help you and your partner define together what is off-limits during disagreements—so your conflicts stay grace-filled and constructive instead of hurtful. Under the New Covenant, you don't have to rely on perfect self-control or endless rules. Because Christ has already forgiven you completely and made you new (2 Corinthians 5:17), you are free to choose words and actions that build up rather than tear down. Grace empowers you to honor each other even when emotions run high (Ephesians 4:29–32).

This isn't law to perform; it's a heart covenant reflecting how grace teaches us to love (Titus 2:11–12). When we fall short, Christ's blood covers, and we can run to forgiveness together.

Step 1: Individually

On your own, write down behaviors you consider unacceptable during an argument. Think about what would hurt your heart deeply or make reconciliation harder. Be honest—no judgment here. Grace covers every past mistake.

Examples might include:

- Name-calling or sarcasm
- Bringing up old hurts ("You always..." "You never...")
- Yelling or raising voices
- Walking away and refusing to talk
- Blaming or attacking character
- Mocking or rolling eyes
- Bringing up family members in a hurtful way
- Bring up old hurts or disagreements that have been resolved
- Stonewalling (shutting down completely)

1. ____________________________________
2. ____________________________________
3. ____________________________________
4. ____________________________________
5. ____________________________________
6. ____________________________________
7. ____________________________________
8. ____________________________________
9. ____________________________________

Step 2: Share and combine

Come together and share your lists. Listen without defending or debating. Then create one combined list of "We will never…" rules that you both agree on. Keep it to 8–10 items so it's realistic and memorable.

Step 3: Add "We will never…" commitments

1. We will never
2. We will never
3. We will never
4. We will never
5. We will never
6. We will never
7. We will never
8. We will never
9. We will never
10. We will never

Now add positive commitments—what you want to do instead. These reflect grace in action.

1. We will always
2. We will always
3. We will always
4. We will always

5. We will always ______________________________

____

6. We will always ______________________________

____

7. We will always ______________________________

____

8. We will always ______________________________

____

9. We will always ______________________________

____

10. We will always ______________________________

____

Out of your combined list, you could formulate a list of Covenant Rules for Conflict Resolutions, an example of which follows:

COVENANT RULES FOR RESOVLING CONFLICT AND TENSION

(Use this as inspiration. Make yours personal)

We will never:

- Call each other names or use sarcasm to hurt.
- Yell or raise our voices in anger.
- Bring up past offenses that have already been forgiven.
- Use "always" or "never" accusations.
- Walk away and refuse to talk (stonewall).
- Mock, ridicule, or roll our eyes at each other.
- Blame or attack each other's character.
- Involve family members in a hurtful way during conflict.
- Go to bed angry without at least reconnecting briefly.
- Let contempt or bitterness take root.

We will always

- Start by praying together (even briefly) for soft hearts.
- Speak truth in love using "I feel..." statements.
- Listen attentively and reflect back what we hear.
- Take responsibility for our own part ("I'm sorry I...").
- Forgive quickly, as Christ forgave us (Colossians 3:13).
- Reaffirm our love before the conversation ends (hug, "I love you").
- Choose to see each other as heirs together of the grace of life (1 Peter 3:7).
- End with touch and prayer to restore closeness.
- Seek godly counsel if we keep getting stuck on the same issue.
- Rest in Christ's finished work so grace covers what we can't fix perfectly.

Signed: ______________________________ ______________________________

Date: ________________

Grace discussion prompts after creating your list

- How does knowing you're already forgiven in Christ help you stay tender during conflict?
- Which "never" rule feels hardest right now? How can grace help you grow there?
- Which "always" commitment excites you most? Pray together about one you want to lean into.

You won't keep these rules perfectly, no one does. That's okay. Christ's grace covers every failure (Romans 8:1). The list isn't a law to obey in your own strength; it's a grace-filled reminder of how you want to love each other. When you fall short, run to the cross together, receive forgiveness, and start fresh. Over time, as you rest in His finished work, the Holy Spirit naturally produces kindness, patience, and self-control (Galatians 5:22–23) in your conflicts.

This becomes a living covenant—not rigid rules, but a shared heart desire to honor Christ in how you handle tension.

EXERCISE FOUR

PROBING QUESTIONS

This exercise gives you and your partner a safe space to reflect honestly on how conflict was handled in your past and how it might show up in your future marriage. These questions are not about judging or fixing each other—they are about bringing things into the light so God's grace can heal, renew, and prepare you.

Past patterns lose power in the finished work (2 Cor. 5:17). Grace renews minds (Rom. 12:2) and empowers new responses.

Under the New Covenant, you don't have to carry old patterns or wounds into your marriage. Christ's finished work has already broken every chain of the past (2 Corinthians 5:17). You are new creations in Him—forgiven, accepted, and complete (Colossians 2:10). As you answer these questions, rest in that truth. There is no condemnation for anything in your history (Romans 8:1). Grace covers it all and empowers fresh starts.

Answer these on your own first, then share openly and listen with grace, no defending, correcting, or debating. Just receive what your partner shares with kindness.

1. How was conflict resolved in your family of origin? (Think about your parents/caregivers: Did people yell? Shut down? Avoid talking? Apologize quickly? Hold grudges? Stay silent for days?)

____

____

____

____

____

2. Has unresolved conflict from your past (family, previous relationships, etc.) hurt or affected you in any way? How? (Example: do you fear anger? Tend to shut down? Feel you must "keep the peace" at all costs? Struggle during tension?)

____

____

____

____

____

____

3. Do you have trouble admitting fault or saying, "I'm sorry"? Why do you think that is? Does your partner seem to have trouble with this? (Be gentle, no blame here.)

____

____

____

4. Do you or your partner have trouble expressing forgiveness or letting go of past hurts? What makes forgiveness feel hard sometimes?

____

____

____

5. What are the biggest areas of conflict or tension in your relationship right now? (Be specific—money, time together, in-laws, communication style, etc.)

____

____

____

____

6. How do you plan to handle these issues, so they don't keep coming up again and again? (Think grace: How can resting in Christ's finished work help? How can the Holy Spirit produce patience and quick forgiveness? What small grace-filled step could you take together?)

____

____

____

Close in prayer together: "Lord Jesus, thank You that we are new creations in You. Heal any old patterns, renew our minds, and teach us to fight for oneness instead of against each other. Let Your grace produce patience and quick forgiveness in us. Amen."

Cutting the Apron Strings

If you don't leave, you can't cleave.

Leaving And Cleaving

Therefore a man shall leave his father and his mother and hold fast to his wife, and they shall become one flesh." (Genesis 2:24)

Jesus and Paul both reaffirm this truth (Mark 10:7–8; Ephesians 5:31) because marriage is meant to reflect Christ's exclusive, unbreakable love for His bride — with no divided loyalty. God gave this instruction at the very beginning of marriage, and He repeated it three times in Scripture: through the Father (Genesis 2:24), the Son (Mark 10:7–8), and the Holy Spirit (Ephesians 5:31). It is not a suggestion; it is God's clear design for oneness in marriage.

LEAVING

Leaving is the first step toward genuine intimacy. When two people marry, they each leave their parents — physically, emotionally, and financially — to form a new, unbreakable union with each other. This new "one flesh" relationship is meant to last a lifetime, reflecting the unbreakable covenant love between Christ and His church (Ephesians 5:31–32).

Under grace, leaving is not something you have to achieve perfectly in your own strength. Because you are already fully loved, accepted, and complete in Christ (Colossians 2:10; Ephesians 1:6), you are free to step into this new union without fear or guilt. Grace empowers you to honor your parents while making your spouse your primary human loyalty. Failing to leave can hinder oneness, but grace covers every past attachment or wound. Christ has already broken every chain (2 Corinthians 5:17). As you rest in His finished work, the Holy Spirit helps you release old ties and cleave to your spouse with joy and freedom.

Leaving is a process, not a one-time event. It is grace-empowered, not self-effort. As you abide in Christ's love (John 15:4–5), the Spirit produces the freedom and courage needed. It often begins years before marriage as you grow toward independence, but it is completed when you fully establish your own home under God's grace. This doesn't mean abandoning your parents — it means redefining the relationship from "child" to "adult son/daughter" and prioritizing your new family unit.

1. Leaving Physically

Living under the same roof as parents or in-laws after marriage often creates subtle control or comparison and almost always creates tension. God's design is for you to establish your own independent home. When you move out, take all your belongings — don't live between two houses. Grace gives you courage to make this step, knowing Christ is your true security, not your parents' home or approval.

2. Leaving Emotionally

Many couples move far away physically but remain emotionally tied to their parents. They seek approval, fear disappointing parents, or carry unresolved hurts that affect their marriage. Grace invites you to bring every past wound to the cross—Christ has already healed and forgiven (Isaiah 53:5; Colossians 2:14). As you rest in His unconditional love, you are freed to love your spouse without needing parental validation.

Three key questions help you leave emotionally in a healthy way:

Question 1: Did I receive my family's blessing?

Some people grow up without hearing words of love, acceptance, or affirmation from parents. This can leave a deep longing that spills into marriage. Grace has good news: your Heavenly Father has already blessed you fully in Christ (Ephesians 1:3). You are His beloved child. If you missed your earthly parents' blessing, receive it from God now — He says over you, "You are My child, whom I love; with you I am well pleased" (Matthew 3:17). Rest in that blessing, and it frees you to love your spouse without needing to earn theirs.

Question 2: As I am leaving home, am I honoring or dishonoring my father and mother?

"Honor your father and mother... that it may go well with you" (Deuteronomy 5:16; Ephesians 6:2–3). Honor doesn't mean blind obedience after marriage — it means respect, gratitude, and kindness, even if parents were imperfect. Grace helps you forgive past hurts and choose honor, knowing God blesses those who honor parents.

Question 3: Where do my ultimate loyalties lie?

Your primary loyalty now shifts to your spouse — you become one flesh. This doesn't mean abandoning parents; it means your new family unit comes first. Resting in Christ's love frees you from needing to repeat old patterns or prove anything to parents.

3. Leaving Financially

Accepting ongoing financial help from parents often creates strings — control, expectations, or guilt. Grace gives wisdom to live within your means and stand independently as a couple. Trust God as your Provider (Philippians 4:19); financial independence reflects resting in His supply, not parents'.

Grace-Guided Principles for Leaving While Maintaining a Good Relationship with Parents and In-Laws

These aren't rigid laws but grace-guided principles to honor parents while protecting oneness.

- Accept parents as imperfect people who did their best with what they knew. Grace covers every wound — forgive freely as Christ forgave you.
- Your primary human loyalty now belongs to your spouse. Grace frees you to love parents deeply without divided allegiance.
- You now have full authority in your own home under God. Parents become honored guests, not decision-makers.
- Your marriage priorities (time, decisions, values) come first. Grace helps you set kind, clear boundaries.
- As parents age, grace empowers you to give them respect, gratitude, and love, valuing their stories and experience.

Leaving is God's gift; it makes cleaving possible. As you rest in Christ's finished work, grace empowers you to leave with honor and freedom, so you can fully cleave to your spouse and become one flesh in joy.

CLEAVING

When you leave your parents and cleave to each other, God does something miraculous: "the two shall become one flesh" (Genesis 2:24; Mark 10:8; Ephesians 5:31). This is not just a nice idea — it is God's declaration over your marriage. In Christ's finished work, He has already made oneness possible. Just as Christ and the church are one (Ephesians 5:31–32), you become one in Him. Grace reveals and deepens this union day by day.

Here are grace-filled ways cleaving grows in your marriage:

1. **Forsake all others.**

Marriage is an exclusive union. Grace frees you to let go of all previous romantic ties. Christ has given you a new heart and new desires (2 Corinthians 5:17). Rest in His love, and the pull of old ties loses its power.

2. **Remain pure sexually.**

The marriage bed is a place of mutual delight and service (1 Corinthians 7:3–5). Grace guards purity—not through rules alone, but because you are already satisfied in Christ. The Holy Spirit produces self-control (Galatians 5:23).

3. **Love is for the long term.**

Grace makes "sticking" joyful, not burdensome. Choose your love, then love your choice—day after day, resting in His unchanging faithfulness.

4. **Live within your financial means.**

Grace gives wisdom to live simply and trust God as your Provider (Philippians 4:19). When you rest in Christ's supply, anxiety loses its grip.

5. **Forgive and forget.**

Grace empowers forgiveness — not because the other deserves it, but because Christ forgave you completely (Ephesians 4:32; Colossians 3:13). Quick forgiveness keeps love flowing and oneness intact.

6. **Make God the foundation of your marriage.**

The strongest marriages are built on living for God together. When Jesus is the center, He draws you closer to each other as you draw closer to Him. Grace makes this easy: rest in His love, seek Him together, and watch oneness deepen naturally.

Cleaving is God's gift — it becomes richer as you rest in Christ's finished work. Grace sustains the bond, produces love that lasts, and keeps you joined together in joy. As heirs together of the grace of life (1 Peter 3:7), you cleave not by striving, but by abiding in the One who holds you both.

AND THE TWO SHALL BECOME ONE

When you leave your parents and cleave to each other, God does something miraculous: "the two shall become one flesh" (Genesis 2:24; Mark 10:8; Ephesians 5:31). This is not just a nice idea—it is God's declaration over your marriage. In Christ's finished work, He has already made oneness possible. Just as Christ and the church are one (Ephesians 5:31–32), you become one in Him. Grace reveals and deepens this union day by day.

1. **Intimate Union**

Marriage creates a new, intimate bond unlike any other. You are no longer two separate people—you are one in God's eyes. This oneness touches every part of life: spiritually, emotionally, intellectually, volitionally, socially, and physically. Grace makes this intimacy safe and joyful. Because you are already complete in Christ (Colossians 2:10), you don't have to cling out of fear or need. You can open your hearts freely, knowing His love holds you both.

2. **Exclusive Union**

God says, "What God has joined together, let no one separate" (Mark 10:9). Your marriage is exclusive. Grace frees you from old romantic ties or distractions. Christ's love satisfies you fully, so you can give yourselves completely to your spouse without reservation.

3. **Symbolic Union**

Marriage is a living picture of Christ and the church. As the husband loves sacrificially and the wife respects and partners, you reflect the gospel in your home. This isn't about rigid roles you must perform; it's about grace empowering you to mirror the gospel. Your marriage is a love triangle with Jesus at the top. When you both draw nearer to Him, He draws you closer to each other. Rest in His presence together and watch oneness deepen naturally.

FOOD FOR THOUGH

God declares you one flesh the moment you marry. You don't have to create oneness through effort or perfection. Rest in Christ's finished work—He has already joined you. As you abide in Him, grace produces the intimacy, exclusivity, and unity you long for. Your marriage becomes a testimony: two imperfect people made one by the perfect love of Jesus.

EXERCISE ONE

This exercise helps you and your partner see how much you have (or haven't) emotionally, financially, and relationally left your parents' home. It is not about judging anyone or proving you're "doing it right." Under grace, your value and security don't depend on how perfectly you've left home. You are already fully loved, accepted, and complete in Christ (Colossians 2:10; Ephesians 1:6). This exercise simply shines light on where grace can bring more freedom and help you cleave more fully to each other.

(Use the rating table you provided — 0 = No dependence / Fully independent to 5 = Total dependence / Still very tied. Include the categories: Financial dependence, Social dependence, Emotional dependence, Acceptance and Approval, Loyalty, etc.)

After rating on your own, come together and share your scores openly. Listen without correcting, defending, or judging — just receive what the other person says with grace.

No Dependence / Fully Independent							Total Dependence / Still very tied in this area					
						Yourself						
0	1	2	3	4	5	Financial dependence	0	1	2	3	4	5
0	1	2	3	4	5	Social dependence	0	1	2	3	4	5
0	1	2	3	4	5	Emotional dependence	0	1	2	3	4	5
0	1	2	3	4	5	Acceptance and Approval	0	1	2	3	4	5
0	1	2	3	4	5	Loyalty	0	1	2	3	4	5

No Dependence / Fully Independent							Total Dependence / Still very tied in this area					
						Your Partner						
0	1	2	3	4	5	Financial dependence	0	1	2	3	4	5
0	1	2	3	4	5	Social dependence	0	1	2	3	4	5
0	1	2	3	4	5	Emotional dependence	0	1	2	3	4	5
0	1	2	3	4	5	Acceptance and Approval	0	1	2	3	4	5
0	1	2	3	4	5	Loyalty	0	1	2	3	4	5

Discussion prompts:

- Where do you see the biggest differences between your scores? How might those differences reflect God's unique design in each of you?
- In which areas do you feel you have already left well? Thank God together for His grace in those places.
- In which areas do you still sense some dependence or tie? How can resting in Christ's finished work—knowing you are already fully accepted and secure in Him — help you release those ties more fully?
- Does your relationship have your parents' blessing? If not, how can you honor your parents while still prioritizing your marriage under grace?
- What small, grace-filled boundary or step could you take together to strengthen your cleaving?

Close in prayer together:

"Lord Jesus, thank You that we are already one in You. Help us rest in Your finished work so we can leave old ties behind and cleave to each other with joy and freedom. Give us grace to honor our parents while making our marriage the priority You designed. Amen."

EXERCISE TWO

This exercise helps you and your partner talk openly about how you will handle family relationships after marriage, especially when parents or in-laws have opinions, expectations, or involvement. Under grace, you don't have to have perfect answers right now. You are already fully loved and accepted in Christ (Ephesians 1:6), so you can discuss these questions from a place of security, not fear or pressure.

Answer these on your own first, then come together to share and listen. No judging, correcting, or debating, just receive what your partner says with kindness and grace.

1. How will you respond if your parents (or in-laws) say something negative about your spouse?

____

____

____

____

____

2. How and where will you spend your first Christmas and Easter holidays?

____

____

____

____

____

3. What have you done in the last month to show appreciation to your parents? What small ways could you show love and gratitude moving forward?

____

____

____

____

____

4. What emotional ties with your parents interfere (or could become a problem) in your relationship? How might grace help release those ties? (Be honest: seeking approval, fear of disappointing them, carrying old hurts, feeling responsible for their happiness, etc. How might grace help release those ties?)

____

____

____

____

____

____

____

____

____

5. Would you consider borrowing money from either set of parents? Why or why not

____

____

____

____

____

After sharing:

- Thank each other for being honest. Celebrate any areas where you already feel freedom or alignment.
- Discuss: How does resting in Christ's finished work help you set kind, clear boundaries with parents? What is one small, grace-filled boundary or habit you could start now?

Close in prayer: "Lord Jesus, thank You that we are already one in You. Help us rest in Your grace so we can honor our parents and fully cleave to each other. Give us wisdom for boundaries, freedom from old ties, and love that reflects Your heart. Amen."

Money, Money, Money

"A budget is telling your money where to go instead of wondering where it went." — Dave Ramsey

Who Makes it and Who Gets to Spend it

Money touches every part of life, and it can cause more arguments in marriage than almost anything else. Jesus talked about money more than He talked about heaven and hell combined because He knew it reveals where our trust lies. When we see God as our source, we stop striving for security in money and start stewarding from gratitude and trust. Under the New Covenant, money is no longer a heavy burden. Jesus finished the work of the Cross, so we can live free—free from worry, free from greed, and free to enjoy God's generous provision.

The Bible gives us a magnificent framework for managing money—not as "owners," but as "stewards" of what He gives us, since we are His and everything we have belongs to Him. We get to live in the abundance of His grace, mercy, love, and provision.

God never meant for us to find our happiness in things. True riches are the treasures we store in heaven: "For where your treasure is, there your heart will be also" (Matthew 6:21). But we do need money to live on earth, so the two of you need to talk openly about it before you marry. That simple conversation can save years of stress and help you build a marriage that rests in the finished work of the Cross.

Because you come from different backgrounds, you probably see money very differently. One of you might lean toward spending quickly while the other wants to save every penny. These differences are normal, but under grace they don't have to cause fights. Instead, they become opportunities to trust Jesus together as your Provider and to help each other grow.

Some of us are "spenders." We think, "If I just had a little more, I'd be happy." That's a lie the world tells us. The truth is, no amount of stuff will ever satisfy our hearts—only Jesus can. 1 John 2:15-17 reminds us not to love the world or the things in it. If one of you tends to spend quickly on things you see and want right away, the other can gently help keep things balanced. But this is never about control or shame. Under the New Covenant, you can dream together, plan together, pray together, and remind each other that Jesus has already supplied everything you need. God gives you the power to create wealth as you rest in what He has done (Deuteronomy 8:18 lived under grace). When you both agree on a plan, the spender learns contentment and the whole marriage feels lighter and freer. Spending then becomes planned and freeing—a "win."

Others are "savers." We think, "If I just save more, I'll feel safe." Again, that puts our trust in a bank balance instead of in our heavenly Father. 1 Timothy 6:17-19 tells us to put our hope in God, who richly gives us everything to enjoy, and to be generous with what He gives. Both spending too much and hoarding too much show we are still trying to find security in money instead of in the finished work of the Cross. God calls us to be good stewards, not because we have to prove anything, but because He has already made us rich in Christ. We manage money from a place of rest and gratitude, not fear. As we stay connected to Jesus, His grace actually gives us the power to be wise with money without turning it into an idol.

Here are some practical things to talk about together before you say, "I do." Pray about each one and decide as a team. These are not laws to follow—Christ fulfilled the law. They are grace-guided ways to honor God as Provider and each other as one flesh. When we fall short, grace covers (1 John 1:9).

1. **Give first from your hearts** (more on this below). Make giving the very first line in your budget because it flows from love, not duty. Giving isn't tithing under law; it's a cheerful response to grace (2 Corinthians 9:7). Start where the Spirit leads—God multiplies what we give from rest.

2. **Choose who will handle the day-to-day bills**. It can be either of you—whichever one is better with numbers or has more time. Dave Ramsey calls it the "Nerd" and "Free Spirit." Usually these two marry each other, which can become great since one has the discipline for numbers and the other makes sure life doesn't become boring! The final big decisions are always made together in prayer. This keeps both of you involved and removes any feeling that one person is "in charge" of everything.

3. **You become one in the flesh, in the bedroom** (ooh-la-la), but ALSO in your financial lives. It's not "my money" or "your money"—it's "our money." Plan, earn, pay, spend, and play together. But don't combine finances until you say, "I do.".

4. **Plan to have some "fun money" to spend without asking.** This removes pressure and lets each person feel respected and trusted.

5. **Be kind and thoughtful if one of you stops working after marriage.** Plan such a life choice together. It will take sacrifice, but coming home from a long day and opening the door to a delicious home-cooked meal can be wonderful! Remember: "We" are earning, planning, saving, spending, paying, and building our dream life dream together.

6. **Put both paychecks into one joint account.** Plan to live on less than you make. There is no other way to grow and dream for big vacations, a home, or retirement. It gives you breathing room if life changes, like having a baby or one of you needing to step away from work. One account reflects oneness—no "mine/yours." Living below your means is trusting in God's supply (Philippians 4:19), creating room for dreams and generosity.

7. **Save up for big things instead of using credit cards.** This builds patience and trust in God's timing. The Bible warns that the borrower is slave to the lender (Proverbs 22:7). Debt often stems from fear or impatience—grace teaches patience and trusting in God's timing.

8. **Decide together what your lifestyle will look like.** Don't try to keep up with friends or family. Your home and life can be simple and full of joy because Jesus is your treasure. Remember that your parents or family might own a nice big house now, but it took them decades to get there. Start small and grow into the future today by not robbing your future.

9. **Choose to be content with what you have.** Like Paul says in Philippians 4:11-13 "I have learned to be content in any situation." Practice saying thank you to God every day for what you already have.

10. **Save a little each month for the future**. Even small amounts add up when you do it together in faith.

11. **Plan and pay extra on your home mortgage every month.** It brings peace and freedom faster. A wonderful, practical tool many couples love is Dave Ramsey's Financial Peace University. It's not a replacement for this session: **it's the next step**! Here's a clear look at the 7 Baby Steps, each one built on Bible truth. These steps have helped **millions** of couples find real peace with money, and they will give you a lifelong plan you can use for the rest of your marriage, and it is based on timeless Biblical principles. Like Dave Ramsey says, *"Live like no one else, so later you can live and give like no one else".*

7 BABY STEPS

These steps aren't about earning blessing (it is already yours in Christ, Ephesians 1:3). They position you to be outrageously generous, reflecting how God has been generous to us (Romans 8:32).

1. **Save $1,000 as a starter emergency fund:** "A wise man saves for the future" (Proverbs 21:20). This small starter fund keeps little surprises from becoming big fights. Don't wait, attack this with a vengeance and get that buffer between you and a mini disaster built! Start with whatever you can. Even if it's only $50 or $200 a month at first. Under grace you don't have to feel overwhelmed; just take one step and watch God help you. Having this cushion helps you both feel safer and more united when unexpected bills come. Dump it into a separate account, not your main checking account where you can "accidentally" buy an 87" 4K TV.

2. **Pay off all debt (except the house) using the debt snowball: "The borrower is slave to the lender" (Proverbs 22:7).** List your debts from smallest to largest and attack them one at a time. Pay minimums on everything else and throw with maximum effort every cent you can squeeze out of your budget at the smallest debt until it's gone. The wins give you momentum and joy. Many couples say this step brought them closer because they celebrated every victory together instead of feeling crushed by debt.

3. **Build a 3–6-month emergency fund: This is real peace.** Life happens every day, whether it's car repairs, job changes, medical needs. If you have an emergency fund, you can face life without panic because God has already provided the cushion. It protects your marriage from stress and lets you give more freely when needs arise around you.

4. **Invest 15% of your income for retirement:** Start early and let God multiply it over time. You're planning for the future while trusting Him today. During the Financial Peace University course that you signed up for… (you have signed up for it, right? If not – why not!) you will be taught how to invest to maximize growth and minimize tax liabilities at retirement. This step shows you believe God has a long, good plan for your lives together. And its Biblical wisdom (maybe instruction?) to

5. **Save for your children's education:** Give your kids a head start without going into debt yourself. Once you have a child, start a college savings plan and add to it monthly. This frees your future family from the pressure many parents feel. You're sowing into their lives from a place of peace, not worry. TEACH your children how to also handle money God's way!

6. **Pay off your house early: Imagine owning your home free and clear!** Throw every extra dollar at the mortgage after the other steps. The monthly payments you save can then go toward even greater things. Couples who reach this step often say it feels like a huge weight lifted, giving them more freedom to enjoy life and serve God.

7. **Build wealth and give like never before:** "God loves a cheerful giver" (2 Corinthians 9:7). Once you're debt-free, generosity explodes. You'll be able to bless others in ways you never dreamed. Helping family, supporting missions, or meeting needs in your church. This is where grace shines brightest: you have more than enough because you've followed God's wise plan.

Session 8 is just a loving introduction to point you in the right direction. We strongly recommend you take the full Financial Peace University course together. It will give you step-by-step tools, videos, and a community that will bless your marriage for decades. The course will also teach you a skill that you will use for the rest of your life! **HOW TO B.U.D.G.E.T.**

Dave Ramsy's favorite saying is: "A budget is telling your money where to go instead of wondering where it went."

Under the New Covenant, we are not under the Old Testament law of tithing. Jesus fulfilled the law completely, and now we give from a heart full of gratitude and love. 2 Corinthians 9:6-8 says: "Whoever sows generously will also reap generously... Each of you should give what you have decided in your heart to give, not reluctantly or under pressure, for God loves a cheerful giver. And God is able to make all grace abound to you, so that in all things at all times, having all that you need, you will abound in every good work." That is why tithing (and giving even more, once you're financially stable) are the first line items in our "spending" category.

Thereafter the priority is "the 4 walls", as Dave Ramsey calls it, Food, Housing, Utilities and Transportation. Those you pay first, even when a crisis hits. (It's much easier to get a ride somewhere if you don't have a car, than to move in with people!) The draft budget in the exercise is by no means exhaustive. To begin, squeeze every expense into those categories. It will provide you with an overview of where your money goes every month. Once you've done the Financial Peace University course, after about 6 months, you'll be a budget PRO, and realize that the budget gives you freedom to spend money wisely and live according to a plan, to achieve your goals and dreams.

Grace actually gives us the power to be more generous than the law ever required! So start by giving first, whatever amount the Holy Spirit puts on your heart. Put giving at the top of your budget because you want to, not because you have to. We GET to give and be a blessing for the church and others! You can also give your time and energy cheerfully, just like your money. As you rest in the finished work of the Cross, you'll find that God meets every need and even multiplies what you give.

FOOD FOR THOUGHT

A budget is simply a plan that shows what we value most. When we put God first and live in the freedom Jesus gave us, our budget becomes a beautiful picture of trust and joy. It is not a list of rules to keep; it is a loving guide that helps you both walk in peace every month.

EXERCISE ONE

MONEY PRIORITIES

Circle the answer describing how you feel about the following. Each one marks it separately, without looking at the other's answers. Then compare and discuss similarities and differences. Specifically find items that conflict with each other, for instance, If Credit Cards are Necessary, then they reduce the possibility that Family vacation can be possible.

E = Extra D = Desirable U = Useful N = Necessary

Items	Woman					Man			
Life Assurance	E	D	U	N		E	D	U	N
TV	E	D	U	N		E	D	U	N
One car only	E	D	U	N		E	D	U	N
Two cars	E	D	U	N		E	D	U	N
Planning your family budget	E	D	U	N		E	D	U	N
Renting	E	D	U	N		E	D	U	N
Buying a home	E	D	U	N		E	D	U	N
Pets	E	D	U	N		E	D	U	N
Tithing	E	D	U	N		E	D	U	N
Charitable donations	E	D	U	N		E	D	U	N
A working wife	E	D	U	N		E	D	U	N
A stay-at-home wife	E	D	U	N		E	D	U	N
A working husband	E	D	U	N		E	D	U	N
A stay-at-home husband	E	D	U	N		E	D	U	N
Holiday	E	D	U	N		E	D	U	N
Cruise vacation	E	D	U	N		E	D	U	N
Continued education or training	E	D	U	N		E	D	U	N
Monthly saving	E	D	U	N		E	D	U	N
Long term saving	E	D	U	N		E	D	U	N
Saving for retirement	E	D	U	N		E	D	U	N
Credit cards	E	D	U	N		E	D	U	N

Remember, there are no right or wrong answers here. This is just to help you talk and pray together. Under grace, nothing on this list is "required" to make God love you more. Use it to grow in wisdom, teamwork, and understanding each other's hearts.

EXERCISE TWO

OUR FIRST BUDGET

Write current real figures, per month (if they don't know what they are - guess, record them for a month and repeat exercise thereafter) for each of you and then plan the "when we are married" in a single budget. Add additional categories as necessary, but don't overdo it.

#	Description		Man	Woman	Couple
	Income				
1.	Income (take home, after taxes and deductions)				
	Expenses				
2.	Tithe	(10% of income)			
3.	Other giving				
4.	Housing	Rent/Mortgage			
5.		Utilities			
6.	Transportation	Car payment			
7.		Car insurance			
8.		Car maintenance			
9.		Gas			
10.	Household	Groceries			
11.		Pets			
12.		Personal			
13.		Restaurants			
14.	Other Debt				
15.					
16.					
17.					
18.					
19.	Subscriptions	Streaming			
20.		Internet			
21.		Phones			
22.	Insurance	Life			
23.		Renters/home owners			

24.	Savings	Savings account			
25.		Retirement			
26.		Vacation			
27.	Medical				
28.	Spending/fun money				
29.	Miscellaneous				
	Totals # 1 – Sum (#2 to #29) =				

Note: Income (#1) minus Expenses (sum of #2 through 27) = LEFT OVER

Congratulations! You've now talked through money God's way. Keep building on this grace foundation. You've got this!! Because Jesus has already finished the work! Use everything you've learned here as a strong starting point and let the full Financial Peace University course take you even further. **Your marriage is going to be filled with peace, generosity, and joy.**

Behind Closed Doors

"Whoever named it necking, was a poor judge of anatomy"

- Groucho Marx

Intimacy

The phrase "behind closed doors" means far more than just the sexual intimacy part of marriage. It includes everything a husband and wife share only with each other: emotional closeness, deepest thoughts and dreams, spiritual intimacy, laughter, tears, vulnerabilities, and yes, the sexual relationship God designed as a gift for marriage alone.

What happens behind closed doors is meant to be sacred, safe, exclusive, and deeply satisfying. It is the place where two people who are already complete in Christ become one in the most personal way. Because of Jesus' finished work on the cross, there is no shame or pressure here (Romans 8:1). You don't have to perform or earn closeness—His love frees you to enjoy each other with honor, freedom, and joy."

We will draw wisdom from Mark Gungor's teaching "Yo Mama - The Number One Key to Incredible Sex" (similar to Session 8 in his "Laugh Your Way to a Better Marriage Small Group study). Mark uses humor and practical insight to show how men's and women's brains approach sex and intimacy differently and how understanding those differences can reduce frustration and increase connection.

In the New Covenant, your sexual and emotional intimacy is not something you have to earn or perform perfectly to be loved. You are already fully loved, accepted, and complete in Christ (Colossians 2:10; Ephesians 1:6). Because Christ's finished work has removed all shame and condemnation (Romans 8:1), you can come together with freedom, vulnerability, and delight.

Grace does three powerful things behind closed doors:

- It removes performance pressure—sex and emotional closeness are gifts to enjoy, not tests to pass.
- It produces purity and honor—the Holy Spirit helps you keep this area exclusive and beautiful.
- It deepens oneness—as you rest in Christ's love for you, you become free to love and serve each other with joy.

MAIN POINTS FROM MARK GUNGOR'S "SEX – THE MIND GAME"

1. Men and women think about sex differently

Men's brains tend to be more compartmentalized and visually driven (testosterone plays a big role). Sex can be a way to connect and release stress.

Women's brains connect everything—emotion, relationship, security, and romance. For many wives, emotional closeness and feeling cherished open the door to physical intimacy.

Neither way is wrong. Grace helps husbands pursue emotional connection first and wives respond with freedom and delight. Rest in Christ's acceptance so you don't take differences personally.

2. The "mind game" of expectations and misunderstandings

Many conflicts behind closed doors happen because husbands and wives assume the other thinks exactly like they do.

Men often want physical connection to feel close; women often need to feel close to want physical connection.

"These differences are part of God's good design. Because you are already fully loved and accepted in Christ, you can learn each other's hearts without fear or frustration. The Holy Spirit produces patience and understanding (Galatians 5:22–23) as you rest in His love."

3. Keeping it sacred and exclusive

God designed sex to be enjoyed only between husband and wife—behind closed doors. Anything that brings third parties in (pornography, past memories, fantasies) steals from oneness.

Christ has already made you new (2 Corinthians 5:17). Grace empowers purity and freedom. If past sin or habits are present, bring them to the cross—there is full forgiveness and cleansing. Rest in His finished work so intimacy becomes a celebration, not a battleground.

4. Making it enjoyable for both

Sex should be mutual delight and service (1 Corinthians 7:3–5). It is not about one person's needs only.

Because you are secure in Christ's love, you can serve each other with joy instead of pressure. Talk about what makes each of you feel loved and desired. Let grace remove shame and replace it with freedom and laughter.

STEWARDING YOUR INTIMATE LIFE: THINKING ABOUT CHILDREN AND FAMILY PLANNING

God designed sex in marriage to be a wonderful expression of love, closeness, and oneness. For many couples, this also includes the joy of welcoming children in His timing. Under the New Covenant, you are free to talk openly and prayerfully about family planning—no shame, no pressure to "get it right," and no need to copy what others do.

You and your spouse should explore the different forms of contraception available. Learn together what might work best for your bodies, your health, your season of life, and the dreams God has placed in your hearts. Pray about it. Discuss it honestly. Make the decision as a team, resting in Christ's wisdom (James 1:5).

Do not let family, friends, or social media pressure you. What works for one couple may not be best for you. Your bodies are a gift from God, and He gives you grace to steward them wisely together.

PRACTICAL GRACE-FILLED APPLICATION

- Make your bedroom a safe, honoring place—no conflict, no criticism, only love and closeness.
- Pray together about your intimate life—invite the Holy Spirit to bless and protect it.
- Keep growing in understanding: read good Christian resources, laugh at the differences, and keep learning about each other as the Holy Spirit leads.
- Remember: the goal is not perfect technique. It is growing in love, honor, and oneness from the secure place of who you already are in Christ.

FOOD FOR THOUGHT

"Behind closed doors is where two people who are already complete in Christ become one in the most personal way. Grace removes shame, performance, and fear so that intimacy becomes a beautiful expression of Christ's love for His bride."

EXERCISE ONE

OUR "BEHIND CLOSED DOORS" VISION

On your own, write down three things you hope your intimate life (emotional + physical) will look like in the first year of marriage.

1.

____

____

____

____

____

2.

____

____

____

____

____

3.

____

____

____

____

____

Share with each other what you have written without judgement. The goal is never perfection of what the movies portray.

Discuss:

How can resting in Christ's finished work remove any fear or pressure from this area? What is one small way we can show honor and grace to each other behind closed doors?

EXERCISE TWO

UNDERSTANDING OUR DIFFERENCES

Answer these questions individually, then share:

1. What makes me feel most loved and connected emotionally?

___

___

___

___

2. What helps me feel open to physical intimacy?

___

___

___

___

3. What totally turns me off to physical intimacy?

___

___

___

___

Pray together: Ask God to give you grace and understanding so differences become a source of delight instead of frustration.

EXERCISE THREE

A GRACE COVENANT FOR INTIMACY

Together, write 4–6 simple "We will…" statements that reflect grace behind closed doors. Examples to get you started:

We will keep this area exclusive to just the two of us.

We will discuss the various methods of contraception and keep communicating as our needs change in this area.

We will speak with kindness and honor, never shame or pressure.

We will pray together about our intimate life.

We will be quick to forgive and quick to reconnect.

We will rest in Christ's love so we can enjoy each other freely.

Sign your covenant and keep it somewhere private as a reminder.

____

____

____

____

____

____

____

____

____

____

____

____

____

____

Sources And Further Study Recommendations

This book draws from many faithful teachers who have helped couples build marriages rooted in the finished work of Christ and the grace of the New Covenant. Below are the key resources referenced or recommended throughout the sessions. We encourage you to explore them prayerfully as you continue growing together.

Books

- *Saving Your Marriage Before It Starts: Seven Questions to Ask Before — and After — You Marry* by Drs. Les and Leslie Parrott
- *Better Together: How to Build a Marriage That Lasts* by Duane Sheriff
- *The Purpose of Marriage* (booklet) by Duane Sheriff
- *The Five Love Languages* by Gary Chapman
- *Secrets to Lasting Love* by Dr. Gary Smalley
- *Smart Money Smart Kids* by Dave Ramsey and Rachel Cruze

Teaching Series & DVDs

- *Heirs Together* teaching series by Greg Mohr
- *Building a Successful Marriage* DVD/series by Greg and Janice Mohr
- *Laugh Your Way to a Better Marriage* by Mark Gungor
- *Better than the Big Screen* by Carol Bester
- *The Marriage Go Round* by Dennis and Tina Korte

Online Courses & Practical Tools

- *Financial Peace University* by Dave Ramsey (highly recommended — a proven 9-week course with videos, tools, and community support)
- *Relationship University* by Mike and Carrie Pickett (Charis Bible College)

Additional Helpful Resources

- *Communication in Your Marriage* by Gary and Barbara Rosberg
- *We Are So Different!* by Michael Smalley
- *Husbands and Wives* (various authors)
- *The Penguin Book of Concise Communication*

A Special Note Many of the grace-filled truths in this guide have been shaped by the various teachers that emphasize the Finished Work of the Cross and our identity in Christ.

Your marriage is not meant to be built on human effort or perfect performance. It is meant to rest in the Finished Work of Jesus and the transforming power of His grace. Use these resources not as new laws to keep, but as helpful tools that point you back to Christ—the true foundation of every strong and joyful marriage.

May the Lord bless you richly as you grow together as heirs of the grace of life (1 Peter 3:7)

www.ingramcontent.com/pod-product-compliance
Lightning Source LLC
LaVergne TN
LVHW061203120826
845149LV00011B/1895

9781972677025